STUDIES IN CONTEMPORARY MUSIC

By the same author

MUSIC AND SOCIETY (1946)

WILFRID MELLERS

STUDIES IN CONTEMPORARY MUSIC

DENNIS DOBSON LTD

FIRST PUBLISHED IN GREAT BRITAIN IN 1947 BY
DENNIS DOBSON LIMITED
12 PARK PLACE
ST JAMES STREET . LONDON SW1

ML117
M487s

PREFATORY NOTE

MOST OF THE MATERIAL in this book first appeared in the following periodicals : *Music and Letters, The Music Review, Counterpoint, Scrutiny, The Musical Times,* and *Tempo;* I have to thank the editors of these periodicals for permission to re-print. All the essays have been revised, some of them (for instance those on Debussy and Fauré) drastically; and while they form a collection of miscellaneous essays I think that certain common themes give them together a cogency which, as separate entities, they could not have. The nature of these themes becomes clearest if the third part is read in conjunction with my book *Music and Society.* The essays on Holst and Rawsthorne overlap slightly with material in that book, but not sufficiently (I thought) to justify impairing such unity as they may have by minor modifications.

As it stands this book includes all of my critical writing on contemporary music which seemed to me to have any claim to re-publication in this relatively less transient form.

W.H.M.

CAMBRIDGE
May 1946

PREFATORY NOTE

MOST OF THE MATERIAL in this book first appeared
in the following periodicals: Music and Letters, The Music
Review, Counterpoint, Scrutiny, New Musical Times, and
Tempo. I have to thank the editors of these periodicals
for permission to reprint. All the essays have been
revised, some of them (for instance those on Debussy and
Fauré) drastically; and while they form a collection of
miscellaneous essays, I think that certain common themes
unite them together—a reproach which, as separate entities,
they would not incur. The nature of these themes becomes
clearer if the final part is read in conjunction with my
book Music and Society. The essays on Holst and
Kurth here overlap slightly with material in that book,
but not sufficiently (I thought) for many appearing; such
unity as they may have by minor modifications.

As it stands, this book includes all of my critical writing
on contemporary music which I regard to me to have any
claim to republication in this relatively less transient form.

W. H. M.

CAMBRIDGE
May 1946

CONTENTS

'A TIGHT-ROPE WALKER AND a dancer are the two creatures combined in any artist who moves me. Every new work is a tight-rope stretched above an everlasting track . . . To-day you can see how very cautiously artists like Stravinsky and Satie have to cross the wire that is to be their only way.'   GEORGES AURIC.

'NO MAN, OF HOWEVER original genius, could wish for a greater gift than the rationally developed traditions of the country in which he is born and the race from which he descends. From his earliest years he becomes familiar with a completely organized idiom whose constituents are sufficiently balanced to make it a ready flexible medium for the practised hand. From the first he enjoys the advantage that he need not waste his time with first questions . . . he can say straightforwardly what he thinks and feels, and the terms he chooses will mostly be intelligible to the average of his hearers. The composer who has the misfortune to be born at a time when almost everyone is dissatisfied with existing conditions will feel obliged to display the utmost grade of impatience which he shares with the advanced thinkers among his public. Then tradition, so far from being a constant help, acts as an automatic break, hampering his movements the more as they become more impetuous.'   BERNARD VAN DIEREN.

'THERE ARE NO MORE schools of music, and the main business of the musician to-day is to avoid any kind of outside influence.'   CLAUDE DEBUSSY.

INTRODUCTION

ON WRITING ABOUT MUSIC

'Music is of all arts the nearest to the abstract sense
. . . the most nearly related to Nature: not to its forms
but to its being.'—FERRUCCIO BUSONI.

THERE WAS NEVER A more fallacious notion than the
twentieth-century cult of Pure Music, for the simple reason
that although in one sense all music must be programme
music since it is concerned with human emotions, in
another sense music, in so far as it *is* music, can never be
anything but pure. No one could ever prove (though it
is always being said) that Beethoven is a 'more philosophical' composer than Mozart; there is a real distinction
implied, but it is one that can be made only in terms of
quality and kind of emotional response. We have unavoidably to admit that as soon as we start to use words to
describe the effect of music we are to some extent interpreting in non-musical terms something which is not the
music but which is more or less closely related to it. It
remains for the critic to seek verbal correlations for, or
references to, certain psychological attitudes which are
implicit in the created experience which the music is; and
thus train the mind of the listener to seize on only those
particulars which appear to him to be relevant to the
sincere response to the musical experience involved.
Obviously the distinction as to where exactly the borderline
is to be drawn between what is relevant to the musical
experience and what is not, rests ultimately on personal
judgment; but something parallel to this seems to me to be
true of any sort of criticism whatever.

A word, of course, is something that can be held up for
inspection; it has definable meanings, even though these
meanings may be complex and not reducible to prose
analysis. Yet even though we may know, ultimately, a little

more about the relation of the experience of (say) *King
Lear* to the emotions of 'real' life than we know about the
relation to real life of the attitudes involved in a musical
composition, I doubt if the matter is, in the literary case,
so very much simpler ; and when we consider the pictorial
arts we realize only too clearly how troublesome, rather
than helpful, the element of representation may be. The
whole question comes back, I think, to the problem of
Language. One is bound to use words to communicate
about *anything;* the problem is, how far is it possible to
describe 'feelings' in words at all, and what degree of
precision can one hope to attain to when one is dealing
with such a comparatively unfamiliar language as music.
Neither the literary nor the music critic can find any
equivalent for the experience the music or the poem is ; he
can merely offer clues and pointers. The music critic's task
is the more difficult, simply because the language of music
is more remote, and because no acceptable technique of
analysis has as yet been adequately developed.

Willy-nilly, then, the music critic is forced to a compromise. On the one hand, he may 'account for' the music
in terms of the established technical jargon—account for
it as a matter of second subjects, developments and inver-
sions, which method is useless as a means towards
value-judgments (and they are the ultimate end of
criticism) and is only in a very limited sense a help towards
understanding and appreciation ; or, on the other hand—
at the further extreme—he may substitute for the composer's music a poem, or rather a prose-fiction, of his own
creation which he imagines to be a literary version of
whatever it was the composer 'meant'. The first of these
alternatives is unhelpful ; the second is both unhelpful and
impudent. I suppose the ideal the critic should hold out
for himself is to keep as close to the simple description in
technical terms as is consistent with saying anything
about the sort of experience the music precisely is, and
the sort of value that may be attributed to it.

In a few cases I think the salient features of the mesh
of feelings and attitudes which make up a musical composition may be deduced from a detailed examination of
its technical characteristics, with some reasonable chance
of demonstrating that one's conclusions are tenable if not
unanswerably right. For instance, it is possible to relate a
certain factitiousness in César Franck's technique—the
sugary harmonic clichés, the notorious tendency of his
melodies to droop back with monotonous persistency to the
acoustically weak mediant, their inability to 'grow', the
spurious, because externally applied, logic of the 'cyclical'
formal processes—to a certain religiose factitiousness in the
composer's ways of experiencing. An equally convincing
case can be made out with reference to Puccini : Dr. Mosco
Carner has deduced the characteristic Puccinian neurasthenic emotionalism from an analysis of his melodic
structure conceived entirely in terms of technique.* Dr.
Carner points out (*a*) how the typical Puccini melody (like
the French *sentimental* operatic aria) begins to develop, but
soon slows down and comes to a standstill ; 'psychologically
it is the expression of a feeling that lacks the power to
stretch out in a long melodic sweep, but soon loses energy
and rests before a fresh start' ; (*b*) how the melody, often
in a minor key, is usually built on simple falling diatonic
scale progressions which (*c*) tend to be broken up into brief
phrases by the frequent appearance of the 'final' interval
of the falling fifth ; and (*d*) how Puccini unconsciously
tries to counteract this falling tendency by grouping these
brief (usually two-bar) phrases in sequences which *rise*.
'These sequences have the effect of a forcible screwing up
of melody which would much rather fall', and thus induce
a neurasthenic flush into the limp and spineless mode of
feeling the origins of which have been described above.
'The tired melody', says Dr. Carner, 'is Puccini's most
personal creation and embodies perhaps his finest ideas'.

* 'Puccini's Early Operas', in *Men and Musicians*
                                        (JOSEPH WILLIAMS)

Now this is a piece of textual criticism giving rise to an account of Puccini's representative significance that is, or so it seems to me, unanswerable. It is an epitome of what music criticism ought to be. Unfortunately, however, this treatment seems to be applicable mainly to composers—such as Franck and Puccini, Chopin and Delius—whose work is of a somewhat narrow and idiosyncratic interest. The more profound, complex and 'central' are the experiences involved, the less possibility there seems to be of backing up one's personal opinions with an 'unanswerable' display of critical method. Thus there are few who would deny that Elgar's use of the brass and his sequences and descending sevenths are intrinsically important aspects of his technique; but whereas some think his brass vulgar and his sevenths and sequences glutinous, others think his brass stirringly heroic and his sevenths and sequences ardently expressive. I believe one can demonstrate fairly clearly that Elgar's technique is not factitious as Franck's occasionally tends to be; but it is a much more difficult undertaking to justify the judgment of sensibility that still remains to be made—to explain why Elgar is, as he seems to me at his best indubitably to be, a great composer.

When one turns to such a difficult and impersonal composer as Mozart one can hardly say anything precise about the reasons why a melodic phrase is 'so and not otherwise': one can suggest why at this point or that it departs from convention, but one can do little to indicate the local manifestations of an 'interesting complexity of feeling'. Yet I do not know that this is a difficulty so peculiar to music criticism as it superficially appears. If it is true that what is communicated in a musical composition can only be the music itself, this is equally if less obviously true of a poem also. Because we cannot at present say anything validly critical about Mozart I do not think we should assume that we shall always be unable to.

Connected with this is the problem of quotation: the music critic cannot even put the text before his readers as

can the literary critic. The legitimate function of musical
quotation is, as I have indicated, for location purposes;
one refers the reader to this or that passage of the score
as an example of the sort of thing on which one bases this
or that judgment. But to quote long passages from
orchestral scores is patently impracticable, and even if it
were possible, the impression the reader would get from
looking over the quotation would not be the same as that
which he would get from hearing the work performed.
Music, unlike painting, is an art that unfolds itself in time ;
nor, when you are listening to music, can you go back to
pick up any thread you inadvertently let slip, as you can
when you are reading poetry. Moreover, no two performances of a given work will ever be exactly alike (except on
the gramophone). The presence of the performer, yet
another element whose psychology has to be taken account
of, introduces complications that the student of poetry does
not have to contend with. It is true that the dramatic
critic has to face similar difficulties, but dramatic criticism
is in almost as rudimentary a condition as musical.

Critics nowadays often make a show of being 'objective',
and are so concerned to see every possible aspect of the
case that they forget, or are unable, to have a point of
view of their own. When we have toiled through their
equable impersonal pages we may have gained an iota of
playful æsthetic cultivation, but we comprehend the music
in question neither more wisely nor more deeply. The cult
of objectivity in music criticism, admirable enough in
theory, too often amounts to a refusal—which becomes an
inability—to make first-hand judgments at all. The
important thing, I would say, is for the critic to avoid
being taken in by the bogus or pinchbeck ; to build up his
own criterion of value, and to establish his responses into
some sort of 'organization' which will give him a point of
reference when he comes to approach new and unfamiliar
works of art—a point of reference which thus does not
depend on the application of non-æsthetic and *a priori*

standards. The critic should, of course, try to make allowances for the waywardness of his own psychological make-up and for accidents of circumstance and environment, but nothing can excuse him from the first-hand effort of honesty in his response. It is the business of the artist to respond at first-hand to life, and unless he does so he will never begin genuinely to create : it is the business of the critic to respond at first-hand to the work of art, and unless he does so he will never begin genuinely to criticize. Thus there is even something to be said, I believe, for the musical journalist; for if one can be a really *honest* journalist—this is very difficult—one has gone a long way towards being a good critic. Good journalistic reviewing, I would say, consists in frankly making moral judgments which may serve as a basis for discussion : criticism consists in the analysis and exposition of these judgments.

For all its imperfections and inadequacies music criticism is a serious calling in so far as it is directed to the training of true musical sensibility, as opposed to the spurious sort which the abstract nature of the art sometimes tends to encourage in musical academies. Knowledge is, one well knows, necessary enough, and to it there can be no short cuts ; but knowledge is not synonymous with education. In the relatively artificial and non-creative society in which we are all obliged to live, some sort of training of sensibility, of critical discrimination, would seem to be as indispensable to musical culture as to any other civilized department of art or life to-day.

Musical Times, 1942

The essays in this book, being written in their original form over a period of about ten years, were not, of course, designed to illustrate the account of the methods and function of music criticism given above. They include plenty of passages in which conclusions are drawn without sufficiently specific reference to a musical text ; and some in which there is specific reference to a musical text and no conclusion. But there are certainly fewer such passages than there were before the essays were revised; and perhaps I may claim that I have at least tried to keep in mind the music critic's more obvious pitfalls.

I

ERIK SATIE AND THE 'PROBLEM' OF CONTEMPORARY MUSIC

I

PROBABLY NO OTHER FIGURE in modern music has been subjected to such persistently ignorant denigration as Erik Satie. Fear of responding to something which is genuinely new or disturbing to their complacency has led people with only the most superficial acquaintance with his work to dismiss Satie as an incompetent *blagueur*, an eccentric who wrote odd sentences over his music; whose compositions can be ignored with cheerful irresponsibility or at most dismissed with some such epithet as 'thin'. Actually, I would maintain that Satie shares at least one characteristic with the very great geniuses of history—absolute emotional honesty and integrity and purity of response— and the obvious difference in stature, the fact that he is a 'minor' and not a 'major' composer, is explained by this very honesty, by his being, with a consistency as rare as it is remarkable, 'of his age'. The reasons why Satie stressed purity of melodic contour, scrupulous veracity of means in opposition to the impressionistic flux, the reasons why the texture of his music is so apparently 'thin' and attenuated, are precisely the secret of his peculiar interest and importance.

For 'supreme art', wrote W. B. Yeats, 'is a traditional statement of certain heroic and religious truths, passed on from age to age, modified by individual genius, but never abandoned. The revolt of individualism came because the tradition had become degraded, or rather a spurious copy had been accepted in its stead'. Considered as a symbolical expression (in ritual) of the fulness of life here and now,

religion, whatever else it may be, has thus a very important
connection with art, and we hazard that in a civilization
in which there is nothing kingly and passionate and pro-
phetical there is not likely to be anything superb or
passionate in art either. Satie's music has an almost
documentary interest in that it is completely unreligious
and almost completely unsentimental. 'Je suis venu au
monde très jeune dans un temps très vieux', he said, and
if he is childlike it is because he has the sort of innocence
that matters for an artist, not because he is infantile. It is
his peculiar achievement that, at a time when the dominant
characteristic of the artist's sensibility is isolation, he
accepted the spiritual aridity to which 'cette terre si
terrestre et si terreuse' obliged him, even though he knew
that acceptance meant in the end a kind of death; that he
steadfastly refused to falsify or distort his response to the
slightest degree in an age in which the temptations to
emotional insincerity are perhaps greater than ever before.
For this reason I believe that no contemporary music has
more to tell us about the position and predicament of the
composer in the modern world than that of this slight and
apparently unimportant composer; for this reason I believe
that it is worth while examining the evolution of his
musical idiom in some considerable detail.

II

In approaching Satie's technique it is useful to consider
first the parallel case of the cubist painters. Ostensibly the
cubists wished to impose a 'fresh' order on the objects of
the visible universe, but to reintegrate a world it is necessary that it should first have become disintegrated, and it is
of this disintegration that their painting is ultimately an
affirmation. Yeats once said that it is doubtful if true
Unity of Being can be achieved without a Unity of Culture
in class and people, and while it is possible that an
individual, anti-traditional formal unity—tending to the
conditions of geometry—may be given to the disintegrating

facets of the material world, it is obvious that such a reintegration is not likely to be richly rewarding as a 'way of life'. However this may be, what Satie accomplishes in terms of musical technique is comparable with the achievement of the cubists in terms of visual symbols. He takes the traditional modal and diatonic materials of European music, splinters them up and reintegrates them with a personal vision fresher than that of a world which seemed to him to have had its day. This reintegration grows increasingly rich and subtle as his art matures; but Satie is never a subversive composer. His musical edifice is built of traditional and stable bricks, though they are placed in eccentric combinations and at odd angles. 'Reconstruction' meant for Satie an effort to be honest : he would find no panacea in a revolutionary 'new tonal system', nor in any spiritual Utopia.

Of the early works those associated with the mysticism of the *Rose-Croix* school of painters are the least successful, though we can see that their extreme tenuity has nothing mystical about it, but is a necessary step in Satie's creative evolution. Technically, they link up with plainsong and organum—the disintegrating process is to start with the fundamentals—not in any antiquarian spirit but rather because Satie saw in the impersonality, the aloofness, the remoteness from all subjective dramatic stress of this music qualities which might, with modifications, approximate to his own uniquely lonely mode of utterance. These modifications take the form of the introduction of sophisticated harmonies in apparently inappropriate, primitive contexts, and of a poignant queerness which the sequences of immobile chords, not untraditional in themselves, acquire through being grouped with a 'personal' logic, but without any of the recognized harmonic relationships :

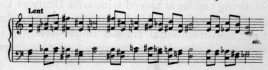

From his earliest days we can therefore observe
that curious impression of a lack of harmonic perspective which Constant Lambert commented on; for
this reason the *Messe des Pauvres,* perhaps the best of these
early pieces, produces in a sensitive performance a sense
of loneliness and helplessness which is paradoxically violent
for a technique so ostensibly flaccid. That the flaccidity is
not due to technical incompetence should be demonstrated
by mere willingness to *listen,* not to mention the contrapuntal economy of the later compositions.

On the whole, however, the *Rose-Croix* works are not a
success; much more interesting are the early dance pieces
—works which establish the formal principles Satie is to
follow throughout his career. In the *Sarabandes* the
sophisticated harmonies of sevenths and ninths are similar
to those in the *Rose-Croix* musics, and they have achieved
a certain fortuitous notoriety because they may have
'anticipated Debussy'. But here the immobile chords are
subservient to a restricted, but extremely subtle and delicate, sense of melodic line. In the *Gymnopédies* and
Gnossiennes the 'cubist' reintegration is transferred from
harmony to line while the harmonies themselves become
the more telling for being simple. This line, if perhaps it
still owes a little to plainsong (of all musical idioms the
most remote from the lush climate of French music in the
eighteen-nineties), is Satie's unique creation, the expression
of a loneliness of spirit that is completely without personal
indulgence. The poise, the impersonality, is achieved partly
by the cool sensitivity and exquisitely 'vocal' contour of the
phrase itself—in the *Gymnopédies* mainly Aeolian, in the
Gnossiennes Lydian and quasi-oriental; partly by the
statuesque symmetry with which the phrases are built up.
There is no development of 'themes', but a complex structure is created by continually placing lyrical phrases,
sometimes of very disparate emotional intensities, in fresh
relationships the one with the other, and by modifying the
character of the phrases themselves through shifting the

harmonic patterns that underlie them. The harmonic unexpectedness has here melodic logic because it is used as a flexible pivot for, and frequently alters the emotional significance of, the balancing phrase (*cf.* in particular the first and third *Gnossiennes*).

Although the idiom appears so fragmentary, nothing could be more highly organized; one cannot alter a note without destroying the symmetry. The balance of melodic periods, the carefully placed harmonic obliquity, the lucidity, as opposed to the impressionist haze, of the tender lyrical phrases, the queerness of personally related diatonic concords—all these give to the music a quality of sunless chastity which, although 'abstract' and apparently tranquil, is acutely poignant and profoundly unhappy. Here, in the words of Jean Cocteau, is 'no noxious emanation, no stirring of the pool': it is the quint-essential music of spiritual solitude. Perhaps the finest of the works of this period is the *Danses de travers,* the second of the two sets of significantly titled *Pièces froides* for piano; music which, in the static impersonal calm of its levelly wavering phrases, incessantly undergoing strange transmutations of harmonic context, its infinitely lonely and lugubrious lyricism, seems to me among the most disturbingly beautiful pages of modern music. Satie's music grew more concentrated as it became more contrapunal; but in such a passage as this we have the essence of his personal vision:

III

Je ne crois pas que d'aller au café, ou en tout autre
endroit de ce genre, soit mauvais en soi : j'avoue y avoir
beaucoup travaillé. . . . Cependant, pour faire montre
de morale, et pour avoir l'air respectable, je dis : Jeunes
gens, n'allez pas au café; écoutez la voix grave d'un
homme qui y a beaucoup été—mais qui ne le regrette
pas, le monstre !   ERIK SATIE

The second of the first set of *Pièces froides*, the *Airs à
faire fuir*, brings us to a discussion of the nature and
importance of Satie's humour. The humour of this
delicately gay piece is partly the *bon-enfant* atmosphere of
the traditional French nursery song and partly the naïve,
simple well-being of the Parisian musical-comedy tune of
the late nineteenth century; and it reminds us of the
typically French element in Satie's art which derives from
the popular Parisian culture that produced Chabrier and
that serves to complement the lonely 'impersonality' I have
tried to describe. Thus the humour in Satie's music would
seem to be merely a trait which any genuine artist must
possess—the exploitation of the possibilities inherent in his
environment. The influence of the period Satie spent in
1903 directing the orchestra at a *café-concert* is conspicuous in much of the music he wrote subsequently, and on
the strength of the salty and tersely orchestrated *La Belle
Excentrique* alone he would take his place with Chabrier
as a composer expressive of the innate *esprit* of the French
temperament, quite apart from the deeper significance of
this work and of his music as a whole.

His Parisianism is more peculiar than that of Chabrier
because he is more sophisticated in the sense that with him
we are more conscious of the critical ironic intellect. To
say this is not to suggest that Chabrier is in any pejorative
sense a naïf. But the perky vivacity of the second *Air à
faire fuir* is belied by a lucidly unsentimental scorn of
cliché in the harmony; and while the direction 'allegretto'

(genre Gounod) at the head of that charming song, *Le Chapelier*, is in a sense an indication of homage, the ironic intention is none the less sufficiently strong to make it clear that Satie knew that the hearty bonhomie of a Chabrier or the unequivocal sentiment of a Gounod could not be for him. He admired their simple-heartedness, but retrospectively and critically, so that the genial French aspect of his art is in no way incompatible with the solitary objective classicism of the early dances. The two aspects are complementary, and it is noteworthy that those singular groupings of lyrical figures and those apparently irrelevant harmonies which are the secret of his austerity are also the means whereby so dispassionately ironic a tang is given to the succulence of his music-hall melodies. There is no feeling of incongruity in passing from the second to the third *Air à faire fuir;* and the out-of-perspective harmonies of the delightful *Jack in the Box*, although more concentrated and of greater linear agility, are directly comparable with those of the very early *Rose-Croix Préludes:*

In the *Morceaux en forme de poire* and the *Quatre Petites Mélodies* (to choose one early and one late work) the two modes are seen to be indistinguishable : here Parisian joviality and indolent melancholy are woven into a music at once civilized in its suave syncopations and primitively solitary in its chastity of line. And we see that the two aspects of Satie are related in him as a man just as they are related in his art. His delight in what he called 'rudes saloperies' was a part of his hostility to the world as he saw it. Of *Jack in the Box* he said : 'Cette pantalonnade me console un peu et sera ma grimace aux méchants hommes peuplant notre monde'—a remark which was, I think, more than ironic.

IV

Between 1900 and 1908, roughly speaking, Satie's music combines the robust geniality of the Parisian *café-concert* melody with the delicate purity of the sensibility 'réduit à l'isolement' in a technique which is, as in the early works, though tonally flexible, largely homophonic. From 1908-16 he created a series of works in which the two modes form a new unity in an economy of technical resource based on the counterpoint of the Schola Cantorum. These works are a reduction to essentials of traditional modalism and diatonicism, so that the music, as well as being a personal re-creation, marks in its technical tenuousness and spiritual climate the end of the great French classical tradition from Pérotin to Fauré—a grave yet quasi-humorous *post obitum*. Melodically the phrases are brief but beautifully pliant, implying an ironic detachment in their poise and in the regularity of the rhythmic periods in which they are grouped. The harmonic texture—which by the time of the *Pièces froides* (1897) had already banished the earlier chromaticisms—is henceforth composed mainly of diatonic concords, the subtlety consisting in the original contexts in which the chords appear, whether as defined by the most stringently supple part-writing or as unresolved appoggiaturas, or even in polytonal combinations. On the comparatively rare occasions when a more complex discord is introduced it occurs at a particular point in the musical argument which re-creates it, gives it a precision that, as part of the stock harmonic vocabulary, it had long lost—I am thinking for instance of such things as the tritones at the end of *Sur un vaisseau*:

the flowing tritone figure in the middle of *Sur une lanterne*
(both from *Descriptions automatiques*); or the relatively
juicy passage at the end of *Celle qui parle trop*:

And the argument is always conducted in the most
scrupulously musical terms : the ironic textual commentary
that Satie supplies to all the 1912-16 series of piano pieces
is a protective irony that arises from the music, not the
other way round. The limpid grace of *Sur un vaisseau,* the
suave phrases and harmonic ambiguity of *Danse maigre,*
the mincing phrases of the miser in *Vieux sequins et vieilles
cuirasses,* the vigorous toccata of *Sévère réprimande* (suggestive of the counterpoint of the early French keyboard
composers), the desolate two-part invention of *Seul à la
maison* (wavering in tonality but clear and ordered in its
melodic periods)—all these exist as music 'in its bare bones'
nor in the delightful *Españaña* is there the slightest hint of
espagnolerie, the music remaining purely French, purely
Satie. But of all these compositions the most consummate
is the *Sports et divertissements,* twenty tiny sketches with
the authenticity of Japanese epigraphs, providing examples
of almost every aspect of Satie's mature art, from the ironic
gaiety of *Feu d'artifice* or *Le Réveil de la mariée,* to the
silky sensual popular tang of *Le Flirt,* to the moving simplicity of *La Balançoire.* The pellucid *La Pêche* also
illustrates Satie's exquisitely musical use of polytonality :

Through all these works the subtlety increasingly depends on the *pattern that is made* out of lyrical fragments, rigid rhythms, harmonies that are in themselves transparently simple. The ease of the writing within the narrow restrictions of the material employed in each piece —two or three contrasted phrases, a clearly defined rhythm, a couple of surprisingly related harmonies—is a triumph of technical dexterity. And this extreme economy of means, this technical veracity, is merely the outward symbol of an inner simplicity of spirit, as is testified, perhaps, by Satie's increasing preoccupation, through this period and subsequently, with childhood. Satie's preoccupation has nothing in common with that habitual refuge of the exacerbated artist, the regression to childhood experience ; rather he saw in childhood an ideal of emotional sincerity which he looked for in vain in the adult world around him. In the preface to *Parade* Georges Auric writes : 'il se soumet très humblement à la réalité qui étouffe le chant du rossignol sous le roulement des tramways', and Mr. Lambert rightly protests against this imbuing of Satie's music with 'a vein of mechanical romanticism' by pointing out that Satie was 'too objective in his standpoint to side with either the nightingales or the tramcars. If while riding on a tramcar a nightingale had flown on to the same seat, he would not have seen in it a symbolization of two opposed worlds and indulged in either philosophy or regrets. He would just have accepted it as a simple occurrence'. This expresses exactly the nature of Satie's childlikeness, and in terms of musical technique his correlations of apparently irreconcilable phrases and harmonies are to it a direct parallel. Like a child he is completely unromantic and unsentimental ; his naïvety is the measure of the impartiality of his vision. Other composers have written music about and for children, but Satie, in his *Ludions* to the poems of Léon-Paul Fargue, has the child's own single-mindedness of attitude. I think it would be difficult to imagine a more perfect collabora-

tion than that of Satie and Fargue. Both have the same
delicate whimsicality without a trace of sentimentality;
but the tender shapeliness of Satie's melodies, the simple
lucidity of his harmonies, were beyond the scope of
Fargue's verse. Satie's music to the *Ludions* and the *Trois
Mélodies* remains crystalline and innocent while Fargue's
poems are, though charming in their ostensible naïvety,
tired with sophistication.

One of the oddest of all Satie's works is the *Trois
Poèmes d'amour,* for which he wrote both words and
music. The verses are a piquantly ironic personal interpretation of the lyric of the *café-concert.* The symmetrical
melodies, both of the voice and of the linearly devised
piano part, use only the simplest and smoothest progressions, with a prevalence of conjunct motion, and the
harmony employs mainly diatonic concords; yet the triads
and lyrical phrases are so surprisingly inter-related that the
final impression is of almost sinister singularity, tender
innocence and mocking irony being woven into a
humorous-melancholy dismay. The sort of innocence that
Satie manifests was not incompatible with the maturest
irony, and it was also a condition of his (within the limits
of his slight sensibility) indubitable moral strength. We
remember the words his friend and colleague, Jean
Cocteau, wrote of him.

> Ecœuré de flou, de fondu, de superflu, des
> garnitures, des passes-passes modernes, et souvent tenté
> par une technique dont il connaît la moindre ressource,
> Satie se privait volontairement pour tailler en plein
> bois, demeurer simple, net, lumineux.

V

Of the works composed by Satie during the period of
which I have given some account in the preceding section
—roughly speaking the years of the Great War—the most
important is the ballet *Parade* (1916). The cult of the ballet
during the war years was to some extent an effort to escape

the self, and much of its appeal lay in an impersonality
similar to that which Flaubert describes when he talks of
'losing himself' in his conception. The new ballet was a
'simplification of current life into something rich and
strange'; as such it was the most lucid expression
of the æsthetic ideals to which Satie and his collaborators
—Cocteau, Picasso and Picabia—adhered. What Satie
aimed at was not, of course, 'pure music', if such a thing
can be supposed to exist, but purity of emotional response.
By shedding the 'human' element, by dealing with depersonalized puppets, Satie and his colleagues wanted to
re-establish their contact with *things*, to respond to things
as they are 'in themselves', not as they are seen through
a too subjective or conventional or sentimental haze. They
tried to lose their personalities in the things that make up
the material of everyday life, and in so doing to render
those things 'rich and strange'. *Parade*, the cubist mani-
festo, was consciously an effort to adapt the ballet to an
end ; its method is explained by Cocteau himself in *Le Coq
et l'Arlequin* :

> Nos bonhommes ressemblèrent vite aux insectes dont
> le film dénonce les habitudes féroces. Leur danse
> était un accident organisé, des faux pas qui se pro-
> longent et s'alternent avec une discipline de fugue. La
> gêne pour se mouvoir sous ces charpentes, loin
> d'appauvrir le chorégraphe, l'obligeait à rompre avec
> d'anciennes formules, à chercher son inspiration, non
> dans ce qui bouge, mais dans ce autour de quoi on
> bouge, dans ce qui remue selon les rhythmes de notre
> marche.

In Satie's score the parts for typewriter, clappers, siren,
spinning-top, tumblers, metal tubes, revolver, empty bottles
and so on may have been ideologically naïve and were
never, it is true, used in performance. But they were more
than the product of a dismally unfunny dadaism : a word
at the right moment, they were literally 'noises' which, like
Picasso's 'objets', were to be transformed into 'something

rich and strange'. Satie himself modestly remarked : 'J'ai
composé un fond à certains bruits que Cocteau juge indis-
pensables pour préciser l'atmosphère de ces personnages'.
It was a perfectly serious undertaking to which Satie
devoted himself with characteristic scrupulousness and
concentration.

As one would expect from the nature of the premises,
Satie's music to *Parade* is the most 'cubist' of all his compositions. Here the re-created 'order' is so symmetrical that
each single movement, and the sequence of movements
that make up the whole, is built on a mirror structure that
gives the work its remote and objective self-sufficiency ;
yet here, within this balanced translucency, are the most
eccentric alliances, the most surprising contrasts of emotional temper expressed in phrase and rhythm—the strange
tonal ellipsis and bouncing ambiguous rhythm of the
managers' theme, the tender *insouciance* of *la petite fille
américaine*, the icy glitter of the acrobats. The verve of
the music-hall lies easily beside the terse counterpoint of
chorale and fugue ; supple lyrical phrases are accompanied
by mechanical ostinatos of the utmost bareness and simplicity, and by syncopated rhythms of a mathematical
monotony. Throughout, the music is exquisitely wrought
and self-contained, yet always intent on providing a *tapis
résonnant* to the steps of the dancers. The orchestration
is sparse and clear-cut, outlining without colouristic trim-
ming the delicate linear structure. *Parade* is still one of the
most important and contemporary of all the Diaghilev
ballets, in a documentary sense at least more important
than Stravinsky's *Petrushka*. In *Petrushka* the puppets are
brought to life ; the essence of *Parade* is that the puppets
are puppets.

The ballet *Mercure* (1924) does not belong chronologically to this period, but may conveniently be discussed here
in so far as it relates—like the *Ludions* of the same year—
to this phase of Satie's work rather than to the compositions
in the 'final' manner. Created in collaboration with

Massine and Picasso, it is historically less significant than
Parade, but still more brilliant and charming. Satie has
described the aim of the ballet thus :

> Ce sont simplement des personnages forains et la
> musique, naturellement, est une musique de foire. Je
> crois que la musique traduira exactement ce que nous
> avons voulu exprimer. J'ai voulu qu'elle ne fût pas
> harmonie de music-hall, mais bien composée des
> rhythmes très particuliers aux trétaux.

The score provides some of the most triumphant
examples of Satie's urbanely distinguished, linear orchestration—the detached calm of *La Nuit,* with its
sinister clarinets, the bouncing tuba of the robust *Signes
du Zodiaque,* the racy sensual tang of the trumpet tune in
snappy *Polka des lettres,* the purity and bareness, without
nuance, of the tiny four-part chorale of the *Bain des
Grâces.* Melodically the music is of superb elegance and
allure ; and Mr. Lambert has demonstrated how the pictorial effect of chaos, in the movement of that name, is
conveyed by rigorously musical means when Satie combines
the suave *Nouvelle Danse* with the *Polka des lettres.*

In considering Satie's ballets it is interesting to remember
that at various points in his career he toyed with the idea
of experimenting in opera—a highly stylized and impersonal art closely related to that of ballet. The idea of
composing an opera on a libretto from *Pelléas et Mélisande*
was originally his, and it was he who, having himself
abandoned the project, suggested it to Debussy. The subject must have been deeply significant to Satie, and he
would probably have made a considerable masterpiece of
it, if one very different from Debussy's. When he died in
1925 he had retired to his retreat at Arcueil to write a
three-act opera on a libretto (by Cocteau and Raymond
Radiguet) from Saint-Pierre's *Paul et Virginie.*

VI

> Quand j'étais jeune, on me disait: 'Vous verrez
> quand vous aurez cinquante ans.' J'ai cinquante ans:
> je n'ai rien vu.   ERIK SATIE

I have now to discuss *Socrate* and *Relâche,* in which
works is manifested the last of Satie's always logical
changements de peau. The difference between the early
'impersonal' pieces and the mature works of the period of
the ballets may be described by saying that whereas irony
is latent in the detachment of the early pieces, in the
mature works irony has become explicit in the incisive
contrasts of phrase, the surprising twists given by a fluid
counterpoint to the most luminous diatonicism, without the
detachment being lessened. Now in *Socrate* there is the old
concern for 'pattern', but not for the bizarre reconciliation ;
there is again no explicit irony. In this work Satie has had
the moral courage to present, without the protection of
any irony, the 'negation' of his life which is the result of
the isolation he had, as a young man, expressed with such
authenticity in the piano dances. Thus *Socrate,* which is
usually supposed, with a certain amount of truth, to be so
completely abstract a work, is really a more personal document than any other single work of Satie's, and it is a
document which cannot but be of interest to any sensitive
and intelligent person of the contemporary world. It is
certainly true that a large number of composers and artists
of accepted consequence have looked upon Satie's music
as one of the most significant achievements of our age and
have seen in *Socrate* a quality of solitariness which is
peculiarly terrifying. On the programme for the first performance Satie had printed the words : 'Ceux qui ne
comprendront pas sont priés, par moi, d'observer une
attitude toute de soumission, toute d'inferiorité'. Few took
this as anything more than a waggish joke, and the titterers
tittered as the composer had expected. If there is any
excuse for them it can only be that *Socrate* is a work of
extreme and peculiar difficulty.

Perhaps the most convenient approach is by way of the piano *Nocturnes* which Satie wrote in 1919, and in which the manner of *Socrate* is affirmed. In these extremely beautiful pieces we seem to find once again a direct statement of the isolation which was embodied in the very first dances, with this difference : in the perfect lucidity of the linear writing a lifetime of experience seems to have intervened. 'J'ai cinquante ans : je n'ai rien vu'. Perhaps this is in a sense a confession of bankruptcy, but only a man of remarkable intelligence and spiritual honesty could admit it in his art as completely as does Satie. Nor is it true in any easy or flippant sense, for this music, despite its 'classic' calm, is instinct with suffering. Formally we notice the typical chastely moulded melodic phrases, built mainly on the vocal intervals of fourth and fifth, with their curious air of timelessness, accompanied by a slowly flowing (12-8) *perpetuum mobile* of uncompromising austerity. Since the writing is genuinely linear the resulting harmony is hollow and irresolute, with a prevalence of fourths :

The sculpturesque melodic phrases are combined together in a symmetrical pattern to form a long unearthly

aria, which is repeated curiously ornamented. Then follows
a broader, more polyphonic and diatonic section of a con-
templative tranquillity, and the aria is finally repeated
da capo. Although this music is so personal to Satie, it has
a quality of oddly sinister inhumanity : it is extremely
disturbing music with something of 'the unpleasantness of
great art'. It is the expression of a spiritual loneliness so
complete as to be almost without consolation ; unless perhaps there is a measure of relief, even of elevation, in the
'terrifying honesty' of the statement.

Socrate presents the same modes of sensibility and the
same technical methods. The choice of the great ironist
of antiquity as a subject cannot have been a mere accident,
but it must be emphasized that there is nothing particularly 'Greek' about the work except in so far as the
sensibility of Satie resembled that of Socrates. Satie knew
that in this composition, into which he put 'le meilleur de
lui-même', he had written music unlike anything which
has been before or since, though it is, of course, perfectly
consistent with his own development. He approached his
subject as 'un acte de piété, une rêverie d'artiste, un hum-
ble hommage'. Once again he makes no attempt to
illustrate his text, and the dialogues of Plato and Satie's
music to them are the æsthetic embodiment of complementary experiences.

This *drame symphonique* is in three parts, the first two
dialogues, the third a *récit narratif* on the death of
Socrates. The music is written in a development of
the rondo form and pursues its course without any superficial connection with the text. The text is sung with each
syllable equally accented, and the melodic lines have the
same static, timeless, expressionless quality as those of the
Nocturnes, with a still greater prevalence of conjunct
motion, interspersed with periods in which the voice
balances on the octave or fifth with an effect of the most
luminous serenity. Usually the harmony is concordant and
diatonic, but it has a strange inhuman shiftiness between

major and minor : occasionally an isolated poignant seventh, or the disturbing entrance of modal tonalities, interrupts the level fluidity (for instance the beautiful modulation at the close of the whole work). By the monotonous repetition of melodic figures and of bare harmonies of fourths, fifths and sevenths, usually produced by fluid linear movement, we are reminded again of Satie's insistence on contour in opposition to the impressionistic flutter, and of a passage in the preface to *Socrate* : 'Ce dessin d'un trait précis et strict, c'est un peu comme si M. Ingres, à la demande de Victor Cousin, eût illustré ces passages des Dialogues de Platon'.

The rhythms are gently insistent, expressive in their very consistency, like a quietly breathing pulse ; the orchestration is superbly devised to outline the transparently embroidered counterpoint. P. D. Templier has pointed out how the various instruments— there are very few—are usually reserved for an individual function : two-, three- or four-part counterpoint for the woodwind (flute, oboe, clarinet, bassoon), scale passages for the string quartet, the harp sustaining the parallel triads, the drums marking the rhythm, the horn and trumpet providing 'curieuses pédales'. In the limpidly pastoral second movement the music seems to be dissolving as the voice floats with tender impersonality over the muffled ostinato of cor anglais, trumpet and cello. Henri Sauguet speaks of the section describing the death of Socrates as 'émouvante jusqu'aux larmes', and the extraordinarily painful effect of this music is achieved while the economy becomes more pronounced, the rhythms sparser and the notes fewer still, the technique yet more apparently tenuous. This simplicity is deceptive. We have evidence of the pains Satie took in moulding and remoulding each phrase, and the integrity of the result of these pains is testified by the fact that the music is utterly inimitable. *Socrate* is, I think, essentially negative music, but it is the probity of its negativeness which is the condition of its strength. I am not trying to suggest that it is a 'great' work, for by its nature it could not be that; what I do want to suggest is that it is an extremely interesting, important and contemporary work which, being expressive of a plight we must all to some extent share, is one which we cannot afford to ignore. It should remain a minor landmark in the history of music, for what Satie has done here with such perfect honesty cannot be done again. When the audience giggled at the first performance Satie's only comment was 'Etrange, n'est-ce pas?', but it was not really strange because people cannot throw off preconceived notions and emotional habits at a moment's notice, and *Socrate* is a composition the beauty and solemnity of which can be appreciated only after long acquaintance. The music of the early dances may be described as the revelation of spiritual solitude through a pure musical intelligence; the music of the period of *Parade* may be called the musical embodiment of the ironic contemplation of that isolation; finally, in *Socrate* and the *Nocturnes,* the irony has again disappeared, and in this music we find the pathos and suffering inherent in the negation which that isolation implies. But this suffering, it must be understood, is completely impersonal and has no reference to any particular private failure or disappointment which Satie may have experienced either at the time of composition or at any other time.

It is for this reason that the 'loneliness' of Satie's music, particularly *Socrate,* is so completely different from the loneliness of the music of (say) Chopin or John Field. Their music expresses the loneliness of a particular personality in a particular environment, in every bar are present the white fragile fingers, the consumptive face, the background of rustling silk and shuttered drawing-rooms. The cool floating symmetry of Satie's music has no such background: it seems as though the music of *Socrate* is present always infinitely repeated, though only when we sit down at our instruments have we ears to hear it. The

music has no human population : the balanced phrases
unfold infinitely in an empty room of which the walls are
built of parallel mirrors. There is nothing to indicate the
passing of time ; it is a very tiny world, but it is self-
reflected into infinity. Its lack of humanity marks, of
course, its narrow limitations, but it gives it, too, its unique
value. There is no music like it because never before has the
artist felt so apathetic—not antipathetic, which is a
different matter—to humanity as to make such a strange
achievement possible. Only a very remarkable personality
could attain to the degree of impersonality which makes
this music, not one man's loneliness, but an aspect of the
modern consciousness, transformed into sound.

VII

Le rideau se lève sur un os.   ERIK SATIE

There is not much I wish to say about that very curious
work, *Relâche,* but I must mention it because it has bearing on the remaining aspect of Satie's work with which I
want to deal. *Relâche, ballet instantanéiste,* was created in
collaboration with Picabia in 1924, shortly after *Mercure ;*
but whereas the latter seems to be related to the earlier
ballet *Parade, Relâche* seems obviously related to the works
in the 'final' style. Here the negation of the final style is
combined surprisingly with authentic popular melodies of
the music-hall, but this time without any explicit irony.
This odd combination gives the work an artificial vitality
with the desiccated regularity of a mechanical toy. Yet it
is hardly a playful or amusing toy, for the music has, in
the rigid repetition of its rhythm, the sinewy gauntness of
its part-writing, its uncompromising orchestration, an
austerity which has become more grimly sinister than
tender.

It is, however, the mechanical nature of the music and
the fact that the work contains an *entr'acte cinématographique* which gives it its importance in that we see here
the final application of the extremely acute and logical

theories Satie had always held about the proper function
of occasional and incidental music. Satie's attitude
to all types of 'popular' music was a completely objective
one and was thus consistent with his attitude to his art
generally. In the charming *Valses chantées* and *Intermezzi
américains* that he wrote early in his career, at the *café-
concert*, there is, it is true, a direct expression of simple
and tender emotion, but even here it is the absence of
extraneous sentimentality and the avoidance, despite the
popular conventionality of structure and harmony, of the
slightest suspicion of cliché which is most remarkable; the
pieces are honestly utilitarian, above all good waltzes and
good foxtrots, without being bad art. In the deliberately
ludicrous *Musique d'ameublement*, and less obviously in the
Cinq Grimaces pour le Songe d'une Nuit d'Eté Satie
composed music which is altogether functional, music that
refuses to illustrate or express but merely provides a background. Such music has not, of course, any value in itself;
but the intelligence of the principle—the concern for the
cleanliness of the tools—matters particularly at a time
when the emotional and intellectual vitality of the 'mass'
of the people is continually lowered through incessant sub-
mission to inferior art.

But of Satie's contributions to the contemporary problem
of functional music the *entr'acte cinématographique* is by
far the most important. Here the music throughout provides a background : it nowhere tries to give musical
expression to the images of the screen, but rather serves to
keep the listener in a state of ready response to those
images without ever calling attention to itself. Melodically
it does not depend on extended themes but on short flexible
phrases repeated in more or less symmetrical patterns,
usually over a mechanical percussion. Occasionally a
broader tune with a popular tang reminiscent of the early
waltzes is introduced, but it remains merely part of a
dynamic scheme, without sentimental or pictorial
associations. The whole effect depends not on the

continuous development of musical themes but on the
building up of a structural mosaic or sound pattern, more
or less underlining the pattern of visual images—a technique the elements of which were obviously implicit in
music of Satie's which has no functional significance.

The writing of music for the silent film was conditioned
by the fact that the musical accompaniment had to be
continuous, so that any of the recognized musical forms
was patently impracticable. Melodic themes were confined
for the most part to very short episodes of the film, and
because these episodes were constantly shifting, it was
necessary that the music, while to some extent reflecting
these changes, should proceed with a certain uniformity
—without, that is, any violent or jarring melodic or
rhythmic alterations (unless of course for some special
'effect') : the music had to stress the inner dramatic continuity of the film, if there were any, and if there were
not it served partially to disguise that deficiency. Satie's
technique starts from and transcends these premises : since
in *Relâche* he collaborated with René Clair, he had an
intelligent and artistic scenario to work from, and he
created a model for the writing of film music which has
not yet been superseded.

With the establishment of the sound-film the problem is,
of course, somewhat modified : since there is no longer any
necessity for continuous musical accompaniment, it is more
possible to write in variations of traditional musical forms,
particularly the more primitive forms such as the rondo ;
and it is more possible to weave realistic sound-effects into
an impersonal and stylized musical fabric. Yet the principles established by Satie still essentially hold good, and
the most intelligent living composers of film music, such
as Hanns Eisler, Aaron Copland, Jean Wiéner, or even at
a lower musical level Chaplin in his music to *Modern
Times,* all betray his influence. The building up of short
linear motives into sound patterns is used by all these composers : there is no attempt at literal illustration, but a

dramatic and visual situation is translated into inherently
musical terms, much as in *Mercure* Satie had discovered
an essentially musical manner of presenting the dramatic
idea of chaos. For instance, Copland's music to the scene
in *Of Mice and Men* in which the big simpleton, wantonly
attacked, finally comes to his senses and crushes Curly's
fist is a directly parallel case, for the music which accom-
panies the wild onslaught consists of a series of explosive
unrelated concords (peppered over the whole range of the
orchestra) which, at the hand-crushing episode, amalgamate
into one enormous grinding discord. In both the Satie and
Copland examples the musical stylization arises from the
dramatic effect and yet is entirely adequate to itself; the
'function' and the 'art' have become synonymous.

What is more, Satie's sparse, clear-cut orchestration
('sans sauce') and clean polyphony anticipate by twenty
years the transparency of tone and outline that to-day the
microphone demands. The orchestra of Satie, who was
willy-nilly writing for the silent film, would be as adequate
for the sound-film of the present as the carefully contrived
stringless orchestra of Eisler in which trumpets, clarinets,
trombones and saxophones (but not the suaver woodwinds
such as oboes and flutes) weave the melodies over a
rhythmic and harmonic base of piano and percussion. The
nature of both Satie's orchestral and vocal writing suggests
that were he living to-day he might be able to evolve a
new form of popular art in a cinematic version of the
opéra bouffe. The chances that a cinematic form of grand
opera—assuming it were wanted—could ever be evolved
are negligible because the film invites too dangerous an
intimacy with the characters. But the enormous vogue of
the film cartoon intimates that there are possibilities for
the cinema in an extremely stylized sort of comic opera
in which the characters are treated as depersonalized
puppets. To such a minor art-form Satie's lucid and
objective technique would be beautifully appropriate; and
his work includes a precedent, for (apart from such an

obvious choice as the marionette opera *Geneviève de Brabant*) his *Le Piège de Méduse* (1913) Comédie en un acte de M. Erik Satie, avec musique du même Monsieur would, produced by such a typically French artist as René Clair, make a superb sound-film almost without adaptation. Musically it is one of the finest of Satie's 'popular' works, of delicious verve and gaiety, and its clean neat scoring— for clarinet, trumpet, trombone, violin, cello, double bass and percussion—would be perfectly suited to the microphone. If Satie's 'serious' music is psychologically a cul-de-sac, his functional music is fruitful with possibilities that remain to the present day unexplored.

VIII

Of all the perplexing problems bearing on the future of music, this problem of the 'functional' is probably the most important, both for the continued existence of the composer himself and for the spiritual health of the people who comprise his audience—the two are really inseparable. That Satie should have been so pre-occupied with this problem is further testimony to his contemporaneity : the probity of the negativeness of his 'serious' music complements the probity of his 'popular' music's fulfilment of a function ; utilitarian honesty is achieved only through and by means of an honesty of spirit which in a world without belief is hard to come by and perhaps a little chilling. It is this insistence on technical and spiritual probity which makes his work so absorbing to contemporary artists : the artists will not forget him though the history books already have and although the only work of his now known to 'the concert-going public' is an orchestration by Debussy of two of the *Gymnopédies* which, completely missing the point, turns them into picturesque pseudo-archaic trifles in Debussy's own early manner.[1] Satie's importance to contemporary artists reaches far beyond the value of his

(1) A very effective and Satien arrangement of *Gymnopédies* for military band has been made, however, by Lionel Salter.

individual compositions. He taught us two great lessons, one the necessity for technical veracity ('l'artiste n'a pas le droit de disposer inutilement du temps de son auditeur'), the other the painful difficulty of that innocence of spirit on which technical veracity depends.

> Les enfants (he said), aiment les choses nouvelles : ce n'est qu'avec l'âge de raison qu'ils perdent le goût de la nouveauté. Instinctivement ils détestent les vieilles idées. Ils se doutent que ce sont elles qui le raseront dans l'avenir, quand ils seront en possession de leur 'intelligence' . . . Tout petit, l'enfant observe l'homme et il le connaît. Croyez bien qu'il ne lui faut pas long-temps pour voir quel 'mufle' il a devant lui.

If we say that Satie 'never grew up' it is patently not with the usual insinuation : towards the twentieth-century world he occupies very much the privileged position that he felt the child occupied with reference to the adult. 'Je suis venu au monde très jeune dans un temps très vieux'.

LIST OF PRINCIPAL WORKS BY ERIK SATIE

PIANO DANCES :

Ogives	1886
3 Sarabandes	1887
3 Gymnopédies	1888
3 Gnossiennes	1890
Danses gothiques	1893

THE ROSE-CROIX MUSICS :

3 Preludes from 'Le Fils des Etoiles' ...	1891
Sonneries de la Rose-Croix	1892
4 Préludes	1893
Préludes de la Porte Héroïque du Ciel ...	1894
Messe des Pauvres (for soloists and organ) ...	1895
Pièces froides ('Airs à faire fuir' and 'Danses de travers')	1897
3 Morceaux en forme de poire (for piano duet)	1903
Prélude en tapisserie	1906
Passacaille	1906

PIANO WORKS OF SCHOLA CANTORUM PERIOD :

Aperçus désagréables (for piano duet) ...	1908
En Habit de cheval (for piano duet) ...	1911
3 Préludes flasques	1912
Descriptions automatiques	1913
Embryons desséchés	1913
Croquis et agaceries d'un gros bonhomme en bois	1913
Chapitres tournés en tous sens	1913
Vieux Sequins et vieilles cuirasses	1914
Heures séculaires et instantanées	1914
Trois Valses du précieux dégoûté	1914
Avant-dernières pensées	1915
Enfantines (3 sets of pieces for children) ...	1913
Sports et divertissements	1914
Les Pantins dansent	1914

OPERETTAS :

Geneviève de Brabant (for marionettes) ...	1899
Pousse-l'Amour	1905
Le Piège de Méduse	1913

SONGS :

Trois Mélodies ('Daphéneo', 'La Statue de bronze', 'Le Chapelier')	1916
Trois Poèmes d'amour	1914
Quatre Petites Mélodies	1920
Ludions	1923

BALLETS :

Parade	1916
Mercure	1924
Relâche	1924

Socrate (for 4 sopranos and orchestra) ...	1918
Nocturnes (for piano)	1919
Premier Menuet (for piano)	1920

'POPULAR' WORKS :

Jack in the Box (for a pantomime) [2]   ...   1899

Valses and café tunes (for voice and music-
hall orchestra)   1903-4

Cinq Grimaces pour le Songe d'une Nuit
d'Eté   1914

Quatre Petites Pièces montées (for small
orchestra)   1919

La Belle Excentrique (for music-hall
orchestra)   1920

(2) Unperformed and left in piano score; orchestrated (very
sympathetically) by Darius Milhaud in 1929.

Music and Letters 1942

II

THE LATER WORK OF CLAUDE DEBUSSY
or Pierrot Fâche avec la Lune

Debussy: 'Mon ciel est ainsi, et non pas autrement'.
Monsieur X: 'Qu'en savez-vous?'
Debussy: 'Je sais parce que j'y ai été'.
M.X.: 'Vous avez été au ciel, M. Debussy?'
Debussy: 'Oui; mais je n'en cause jamais avec les étrangers'.
(Quoted by R. GODET in *La Revue Musicale,* Dec. 1920).

TO UNDERSTAND THE SIGNIFICANCE of Debussy's late work it is necessary to be clear as to the kind of musician he was; or one could say with equal truth that one cannot understand the kind of musician Debussy was without responding sympathetically to his final works. He was, throughout his life, an exile. He had, one must remember, no intention of effecting a 'revolution' in musical history. 'Nous ne sommes pas modernes' he said explicitly, and he made it clear early in his career that he knew he was destined to be an exile, and that if he wrote music it would be for himself and his friends. There are no more schools of music, he thought; and the main business of the musician to-day is to avoid any kind of outside influence! His music was an incessant fight against 'le sentiment insupportable de vivre en ces lieux d'exil où il semble qu'être quelqu'un ne puisse aller sans cabotinage, et où la musique manque d'infini'. Because the outside world seemed to him corrupt he retired into his retreat, became preoccupied with 'la vie intérieure' where alone, if at all, the 'infini' might still be found. 'Espérez qu'il reste des dieux, nous en avons le plus pressant besoin'. Whatever gods Debussy discovered he found within his own spirit, and it is this apprehension of the indestructible beauty of

the inner life which is expressed in the suave, intimate
lyricism of his early songs, and in ways more or less subtle,
in all his finest work.

The songs provide the key to Debussy's most interesting
music, and there was no medium more suitable for the
expression of his sensibility. It is remarkable that he had
attained to maturity in this form while his piano music
was still either incompetent or merely agreeably pretty—
associated with that academic (Massenet) tradition against
which Debussy's representative music is a protest. In a
rather obvious sense the early songs are, of course, 'escape'
music—music of *Fantôme* and of Pierrot, the outcome of
the composer's attempt to seek infinity within himself, his
deliberate desire to see the image as more real than the
object, the dream more real than the waking life. This
dream-like quality is expressed, as Constant Lambert and
others have pointed out, in the peculiarly static way in
which Debussy uses his harmonies; the lush sevenths and
ninths are presented purely as nervous sensation, divorced
from any sense of melodic or harmonic *development;* not
being part of any rhetorical argument, they produce a
disturbing sense of nervous deliquescence.

On the other hand the extremely intimate relation of
Debussy's melodic line to the French language—a sympathetic response not so far from the classical declamation
of Lully and Rameau as one might expect—safeguards the
music's humanity; and it is probably a latent conflict
between the human immediacy of the vocal lines and the
static remoteness of the harmony which imbues these songs
with a poignancy so much deeper than anything found in
the early piano pieces. The dream world of paradisal parks
and moonlit balconies is there in the floating, disembodied
harmonies; but the subtle inflections of the vocal lines,
growing so intimately in their 'natural' pentatonic curves
from the inflections of the *spoken* word, give to the music
a sense of loss and regret, remembrance of life once vivid
and vital from which one is now separated. The vocal line

'humanizes' the harmonies; and the harmonies divest the
line of dramatic tension, suggest a directly 'nervous'
response.

All these modes of sensibility are present not only in
the songs but also in *Pelléas et Melisande* and in the
orchestral *Nocturnes*. In all, the connections between the
inner and the outer life are preserved, even though the
latter may be present only retrospectively; and the technical manifestation of these connections grows out of the
technique of the early songs. The plastic and expressive,
if not very sustained, melodic line of the orchestral works
derives from the intimate lyricism (related to the French
language) of the songs, while the delicate pointillist scoring
is related to the filigree-work of the piano parts of the
Fêtes Galantes and *Ariettes Oubliées*. The orchestral *Nocturnes* are a dream art far distant from the flaccid
dreamings of the Pre-Raphaelites—a pervasive influence to
which Debussy had himself succumbed in the early *La
Demoiselle Elue*. This art is not so much a dream as a
vision, no mere querulous subjective wailing but a vision
of the ineffable loneliness of the human spirit. If the static
harmonies arise from the nervous sensation of the
individual personality, they dissolve away into the impersonality of the forces of nature. Even in *Fêtes* the
festivities are seen retrospectively, from a distance. There
is a significant paradox at the heart of Debussy's work:
art which lives on the nerves of the individual, ignoring
the rest of humanity and society, will end by losing its
'personality' in subservience to the external world. No
music has expressed this representatively contemporary
experience with greater poignancy than the music Debussy
wrote during the middle years of his career, unless it be
the very finest work of Delius.

It is, I suppose, obvious enough that such an experience is by its very nature precarious. The creation of a
private world of the sensibility puts a heavy burden on
'inspiration'. One must write with intensity and con-

viction if one is to avoid the temptation to feed passively
on the sensory stuff on which the imaginations of artists
live ; and I think there were times when both Delius and
Debussy, relying almost exclusively on a recondite harmonic
dialect, were content to be in this sense negative and non-
creative. Delius had to rely almost entirely on his own
imaginative resources, and the relatively low proportion
of passively sensory music in his output can be attributable
only to his genius's paradoxical vigour—considering the
nostalgic, death-tending nature of his sensibility. Debussy,
despite a self-imposed exile hardly more equivocal than
Delius's, was fortunate enough to work in a country which
still preserved a continuous musical tradition ; his development in technical and emotional maturity may be said
to consist in an increasing ability to come to terms with
that tradition without sacrificing the integrity of his personal attitudes.

If one compares *La Mer* and still more the orchestral
Images with the earlier pieces the significance of this
development is clear. Although these works appear at first
hearing improvisatory and rhapsodic, they soon reveal
themselves as most subtle and complex examples of musical
organization. They are at once less static and more linear
than the earlier *Nocturnes; Gigues* (from *Images*) is a more
difficult piece to listen to than *Fêtes* (from *Nocturnes*), but
in the long run it is richer and more rewarding ; its linear
details, though still short-breathed, are both intrinsically
more subtle, and more subservient to a structural purpose.
The terrific vitality of the *Rondes de Printemps*—its
powerful rhythm, its textural lucidity—remind one
forcibly of Roussel and even Milhaud ; Debussy now links
up with one of the central lines in contemporary French
(and European) music, is ceasing to be a figure in the literal
sense eccentric. His growing interest in Couperin and the
classical tradition is evidence of a profound if unobstrusive
modification in his attitudes to his art and experience. As
the late works become better known (they are not, for

obvious reasons, as popular as the early things and have been frequently misunderstood) I think we may see Debussy as a figure of an importance rather different from what we had supposed. We may see him not only as a lonely 'genius' in the sense in which the term is applicable to Delius, but as a central figure in the French tradition.

Already, in the *Images,* Debussy has proved that his remark 'Nous ne sommes pas modernes', quoted earlier, was to be no more than partially apposite; and if the *Images* represent in their range and richness probably the high-water mark of his achievement, the trend towards the contemporary and the traditional which they manifest is to attain a more extreme development in the works of his very last years, in particular the three sonatas. From this point of view, their technique calls for a somewhat more detailed study.

'Retrouvons notre liberté, nos formes', Debussy wrote; 'les ayant inventées pour la plupart, il est juste que nous les conservions.' The composition of sonatas for two or three instruments is itself indicative of a new approach; but what is perhaps most immediately noticeable about these last works is the much greater importance of the melodic element. The first movement of the cello sonata especially shows a hitherto unsuspected power of sustained melodic thinking; and if the nature of the melodic development is more often of a kind that one can call 'short-winded', such a description is not of much value without elaborate qualification. Such a very different composer as Richard Strauss might be described as short-winded in his melodic utterance, but the term would then bear a very different meaning. It could also be used of the melodies of Erik Satie, again with a distinct connotation. Thus in calling some of the melodies of Strauss short-winded one would not mean that their actual length was short but rather that they tended to be too long, that their duration in time exceeded their imaginative life. To call Satie's melodic utterance short-winded on the other

hand, would not be to deny that he was, within his limits,
a remarkable master of melodic line ; his melodies are brief
and symmetrical by the inherent nature of his genius, and
we are not conscious of any frustration but of perfect
realization. It may have been a small thing that Satie was
doing (though it is not as small as it looks) but it was, as far
as it went, completely satisfying.

Now Debussy's melody, in his last works, falls some-
where between these two stools. The duration of his
melodies does not exceed their imaginative life ; as soon
as that is exhausted they abruptly stop. On the other hand
we do not feel, as with Satie, that they are brief because
Debussy wanted them to be, but rather because he could
not help it. They are not symmetrical self-contained
organisms, their life is, as it were, volcanic ; a phrase will
suddenly spurt up, as suddenly subside, another will follow
it, and then another :

Where they differ from the earlier works is in the
manner in which attention is concentrated, not on
the harmonic chiaroscura, but on these apparently fragmentary melodic phrases, with their violent contrast of
mood, now piercing and vibrant, now sultry and
languorous ; so that the earlier direct response through the
nervous system to an harmonic flux, is superseded by a
response which calls in play much more complex aspects
of the mind and intelligence. We see here, in this somewhat
peculiar melodic writing, a subtle and highly developed
approach to a problem of formal integration. This

approach may not bear much relation to conventional sonata development; it certainly makes little use of contrasts of tonal centre and is inherently undramatic; but if we listen sensitively to these works we can no longer doubt that Debussy has solved his particular formal problem with superb assurance and clarity. Thus in the first movement of the violin sonata the tender drooping opening phrase is not 'thematically' developed in the normal sonata sense, nor does it itself lyrically evolve : it is presented in juxtaposition to and contrast with other melodic phrases often very different in mood, and in shifting harmonic contexts, and through the contrasts its emotional significance is widened and intensified. When the simple little phrase is restated in the coda we finally realize how inevitable the apparently fragmentary progress of the movement has been. If the volcanic spurtings of fioritura, punctuating the limp tranquillity of the harmonies, remind one occasionally of something induced by the hypodermic syringe, the precision and lucidity of the phrase-grouping should effectively counteract the superficial notion that this is, in any opprobrious sense, the music of a sick spirit.

The nature of Debussy's melodic thinking in these works shows a most interesting modification of his long-standing interest in the exotic. His sensuous imagination had long been attracted towards the exotic and some of his finest music, notably the *Nocturnes, La Mer,* and *Images* and the piano piece *L'Ile Joyeuse* [1], manifests in its curling

(1) In some ways the quite early *L'Ile Joyeuse* seems to me the most wonderful piano piece Debussy ever wrote. The title itself, with its reference to Watteau, is strangely fascinating, for whereas all Debussy's music may be said to exist in an island—a world remote from the everyday world—the last thing one could say about the world most typical of the composer's imagination would be that it was joyous. The gaiety, luxuriance and vitality of this piece are unique in Debussy's earlier work, its intricacy of ornament, gorgeousness of harmonic colouring and excitement or rhythm overwhelming; it is the world of Carnival, of Pierrot, become magically alive and actual, almost comparable with the outward-turning Chabrier or the ardent sonority of Albeniz's *Iberia*.

D

voluptuous melodic threads, qualities that have affinities
with eastern musics. Usually the exotic element is exploited
decoratively in the creation of Debussy's private world;
but in the final works (where it is partly Spanish in origin,
partly derived from the troubadours and other aspects of
medieval music) it is not used for its own sake, as a 'value'
but is queerly contorted by the other modes of sensibility
the composer is expressing. In the violin and cello sonatas
pentatonic arabesques, taut augmented intervals, and
'Spanish' rhythms abound, but they are no longer used for
their glamorous associations; occurring within the precise
lucid texture and the economical structure they rather
produce a sense of deliberate stylization.

A similar tendency is noticeable in the harmonic treatment in these works. On the whole the harmonies are
simpler than in Debussy's more 'impressionistic' works; the
higher chromatic discords occur but rarely, and considerable play is made with 'modal' juxtapositions of diatonic
triads which often have structural significance in the
repetition of the phrases:

And cf. the odd passage in the last movement of the violin sonata in which the development as it were, 'winds itself up' again after one of its periodic collapses, by repetitions of a brief, tentative phrase at intervals of a rising third ; in such passages Debussy's old habit of grouping his phrases rather mechanically in pairs is given an altogether subtler interpretation). The familiar 'static' sevenths, ninths and elevenths still appear, but being subservient to the melodic element in these sonatas, and occurring in this tight, formal structure they are de-glamorized ; they are no longer 'indulged in', but are used objectively to create a clearly defined, intentionally artificial stylization :

It is not merely that this convention is a narrow one ;
so, superficially considered, is Mozart's or Couperin's ; it
is that it is conceived as, accepted as, an artificial
convention, a convention of puppet-like unreality. Couperin
and Mozart hardly thought of their convention as such
at all ; it was simply the idiom, the criterion, which society
presented them with, and which they could use for their
own ends. But Debussy's convention is not a product of
society ; it is a stylization deliberately evolved for a personal end, and the impeccable lucidity of its realization,
the honest acceptance of the artificiality of the mannered
harmonies, is a measure of Debussy's growth in self-
knowledge. It need hardly be added that the acceptance of a stylization, providing it is consistently
realized, is not necessarily a limitation even though it may
be a personal stylization rather than a gift of the community ; and I think we shall understand Debussy's stylization the better if we see it in relation to his life-long preoccupation with the figure of Harlequin.

There can be no doubt that the mythological Harlequin
exerted an almost obsessive influence on Debussy's
imagination. Watteau, whose 'artificial' stylization was, of
course, the legacy of his society, had imbued his Gilles with
a pale forlorn melancholy which seemed to suggest the
loneliness of the individual even in the midst of an
apparent social solidarity ; it is not therefore surprising that
the more isolated modern artist should see in Harlequin,
the divine Fool, a symbolization of his own difficulties and
nostalgia ; one thinks immediately of Picasso, while among
musicians Busoni wrote one of his most personal operas

around this legendary creature. Now in his early work Debussy accepts the mythological pierrot world, the world of the Mask, as something intrinsically good, positively valuable; at the end of his life, worn out by disease and the attrition of the war, he begins to see through himself, to see that the Mask and the Phantom are not enough, cannot be permanently satisfying; he begins to contemplate them ironically. He looks back on his life and sees it in the likeness of a puppet-show, himself, moon-eyed, desiring but perpetually dissatisfied, in the mask of Harlequin. 'Pierrot fâché avec la lune' was a proposed epigraph to the cello sonata, and it is surely this newly won honesty and self-knowledge which finds its manifestation in the consummate felicity of the technique of these last works, in the consistency of their conventional stylization. Debussy's Mask and Phantom have failed him; and the failure is a new start.

And so, disillusioned though it may be in the strict sense, this music conveys an impression not of spiritual sickness, but of freshness and health. Because of their honesty, these works have dignity and power. Although in a sense topical, and local and personal, although not in an idiom having, like Couperin's, social and religious validity, these works can take their place in a great classical tradition. The purity of the realization gives to music which is instinct with the contemporary *malaise* a quality which we may justly call nobility; the tortured modern spirit achieves here a classical objectivity and tragic pathos. It is indicative of their significant contemporaneity that they should in this way be comparable with some of the later work of Stravinsky.

Possibly the cello sonata is the finest of all these pieces, particularly the first movement which beneath its Spanish-seeming and troubadour-like melodic arabesques has a remarkable spaciousness; although not actually of great dimensions and although in a completely different idiom, it produces an impression of grandeur and of massive

proportions almost comparable with Couperin and Racine.
The extraordinary, frustrated Serenade is one of the most
concentrated of Debussy's Harlequin pieces, and the most
significantly 'modern'. The violin sonata also has a Harle-
quinade instead of a slow movement—conveying the
intensest poignancy through its precious harmonies and
passionate exoticisms of figuration. In the last movements
of both violin and cello sonatas infectious dance rhythms
are allied with—and interrupted by—Debussy's characteristic structural methods with, again, a paradoxical
mingling of clarity with complexity. Other examples
of Debussy's harlequin-music are found in the remote
and fanciful virtuosity of the piano *Etudes* (particularly the one in sixths), and in that most mournfully
vivacious war-music, *En blanc et noir* for two pianos. *Le
Martyre de St. Sebastian* gives an altogether more profound
interpretation to the drugged neurasthenia of the nineties.
One has only to compare the mediaeval elements in this
work with such a relative hot-house plant as *La
Demoiselle Elue* to see how the austere harmonies, the
organum-like effects, the fluid texture of this most lovely
score achieve a lonely spiritual remoteness, a combination
of intensity with objectivity, such as we have seen to
characterize all Debussy's final compositions. The pity is
that the work—one of Debussy's very greatest creations—
is so seldom performed.

Debussy himself thought the third of the sonatas (that
for flute, viola and harp, the last to be completed of the
projected series of six), to be the best. It contains perhaps
nothing as impressive as the first movement of the cello
sonata, but it has a superb unity of conception and in its
combination of an unexpectedly intense exoticism in the
lines, especially in the first movement, with a Watteau-
like elegance of stylization, is perhaps the most representative of these final works. Debussy himself said of it :

'C'est affreusement melancholique et je ne sais pas si
on doit en rire ou en pleurer. Peut-être les deux?

> . . . Rude et belle musique, jamais fausse pourtant.
> C'est d'ailleurs une erreur trop commune de croire,
> quand on déchaine les elements, qu'il faut absolu-
> ment les mettre en rapport de septième . . . Plus je
> vais, plus j'ai horreur de ce désordre voulu qui n'est
> qu'un trompe-oreille, comme aussi des harmonies
> bizarres, qui ne sont que jeux de société. Combien il
> faut d'abord trouver, puis supprimer, pour arriver
> jusqu'à la chair nue de l'emotion'.

The quotation is interesting for the light it throws on
Debussy's attitude to his art at the time, and 'la chair nue
de l'emotion' is what in all these works gives such limpidity
to the texture and structure. Debussy never wrote anything
more perfectly realized than these calmly complex sonatas.
Although in more senses than one *opera ultima*, they are
pregnant with possibilities for future development, had the
composer lived ; and they mark Debussy's realization that
much of what he had previously accomplished was, however beautiful, partial and incomplete.

Music and Letters 1938 (revised 1945)

III

THE LATER WORK OF
GABRIEL FAURE

'Civilization is strength and not weakness. Look at
the great nations of Europe and what they have en-
dured. No savage could have stood the things they
have gone through. It is their civilization that has given
them such moral strength and courage. I do believe in
civilization.'—SIBELIUS.

(Quoted by BENGT DE TÖRNE).

I

IN WRITING OF SATIE I drew attention to some of
the consequences, for the composer, of what one might call
the contemporary attitudes and their underlying socio-
logical origins. We saw in Satie perhaps the most extreme
case of the 'modern sensibility'; yet the integrity he sought
for in the midst of his spiritual isolation has been the
guiding motive of some of the most 'central' of Europe's
contemporary composers also, and Stravinsky's later work
in particular manifests in a richer and more varied form
an essentially Satiean æsthetic. The deracination, the exile
—first in France and then in America—of this great
creator assumes a kind of symbolical significance; but even
an artist such as Schönberg, who after all preserves some
kind of direct continuity with the Viennese instrumental
tradition; or such as Bartók, who relatively maintains contact with a traditional way of life, with a folk culture and
a classical musical tradition, is effected by something close
to Satie's irremediable spiritual exile. This we may see not
only, or indeed mainly, in their moods of revolt, but in
the glassy, tenuous texture which, in their different ways,
characterizes their most mature and significant slow movements (for instance that of Schönberg's Fourth Quartet and
of Bartók's Music for strings, celesta and percussion). We

have little difficulty in understanding the position of an
artist like Schönberg or Bartók who is aware of the heritage
of European civilization but at the same time, in the contemporary industrial environment, isolated, in revolt; but
a composer of to-day whose music is completely civilized,
itself the incarnation of a mode of civilization as well as a
personal expression—as Mozart's was, or even more as
Bach's was—such a composer is too much for us to grapple
with. We do not know how to tackle Fauré, how to square
him with our niggling conceptions of the modern scene;
so that in a sense it is possible to say that his late work
presents difficulties to the uninitiated which more
obviously 'contemporary' composers do not. At his best, in
his mature works and above all the compositions of his
final years, he attains to an intimate limpidity in which
the note of personal accident or distress obtrudes—notwithstanding the individuality of the idiom—even less than
in Mozart; a limpid force which can, indeed, be compared
with the sublime autocracy of Bach. Yet Fauré is, in point
of time at least, in his late work a contemporary composer; which fact suggests that there is something peculiar
about his 'civilization'. It will be the task of this essay to
try to define what the peculiarity of this civilization
consists in.

II

In a way, the civilization that is Fauré's music is ideal;
that is to say it has no objective reality—such as Byrd's or
Bach's or Mozart's civilization had—outside the music. But
at the same time it is not so miraculous a phenomenon
as to be the creation of Fauré as an individual personality,
but is rather the consummation, through this one individual, of many traditional facets of the French
temperament. It may be that Fauré was able to achieve this
because the traditions of French music, and of French life,
have been relatively continuous; because France suffered to
a much less severe degree from the breakdown of cultural

unity, which in Germany resulted in Wagnerism and in England produced a complete cultural decay of which the ultimate manifestation was the Industrial Revolution. The delicate alliance between the religious and spiritual impulses of the artist and the folk which characterized mediaeval France did not altogether collapse, as it did in England, during the rising of urban civilization, perhaps because France has preserved, relatively, an agricultural economy. There is an unbroken line from the troubadours and Perotin to the elegance of a Guillaume de Costeley, and thence to the more ostensibly social and sophisticated Lully and Rameau, and still more to Couperin whose poise and purity, wit and tragic pathos in church music and secular instrumental music, attain a spiritual profundity which only Bach, among contemporaries, can rival. And whereas the Bach tradition in Germany was an end, the Couperin tradition in French music survived, if in a more superficial form, through the nineteenth century; even the César Franck school, the closest French composers came to the chromatic-harmonic self-dramatizing Wagnerian ethos, preserved in such composers as Vincent d'Indy, Dukas and in a different way Chausson, connections with the classical tradition. Debussy himself, the super-individualist, owed his precision and delicacy in sensuous transcription to attitudes unconsciously assimilated from the classical tradition, and in his later years unequivocally paid tribute to its spiritual significance. We are perhaps now in a position to appreciate how much Berlioz's intensity and aristocratic finesse owes to conventions—of line, texture, form and harmony—which are essentially French, classical, and anti-romantic in the Wagnerian sense (despite the ultra-romantic exterior trappings of Berlioz's career); and to see how the wit and refinement of most French entertainment music in the nineteenth century preserves an unbroken tradition from the comic opera-ballets of Lully and reaches the heights of comic genius in Chabrier's *Le Roi Malgré Lui*. That

Chabrier could also write works of such spiritual elegance and tenderness as *Briséis* and the *Ode à la Musique* shows that there was still in France none of that artificial division between the 'light' and the 'serious' which had become characteristic of England and Germany.

I do not know that Gounod was very much more talented than England's Sterndale Bennett; and yet Gounod produced, as well as the *Redemption* and such barbarities as the notorious *Ave Maria,* a work as exquisite and impeccable as *Philémon et Baucis.* That is a tribute to a still vital tradition; and it is significant that in France, despite Berlioz's and Debussy's strictures on musical academies, the 'academic' conventions remained sufficiently in tune with contemporary creative practice for men such as Fauré and d'Indy to hold important academic positions. This is a point of great importance for the understanding of Fauré's art. His music provides a kind of retrospect on French civilization as it ideally might have been; and he effects this re-creation as an artist, a professional musician—more completely professional perhaps than any composer of the last hundred years, almost as completely professional as Bach or Palestrina. He is more sophisticated than these because he *creates* his civilization out of his own musicianship whereas they express their civilization—and of course their personal attitudes towards it—*through* their musicianship. (Palestrina made music in praise of God as a skilled craftsman makes a chair.) But he is a composer of the same genus . If we do not recognize this, we shall find his mature work persistently baffling.

III

The comparison of Fauré's music with Bach, suggested by Koechlin, seems to me more to the point than the conventional comparison of his work with the art of the Greeks. Of course we can see that Greek art must have appealed to Fauré, that he would have admired its concision and sobriety, its freedom from excess and enervating despair; it is even possible that Fauré's own ideal civilization resembles Greek civilization in certain particulars—in its quality of *raison* for instance, a word for which we have no precise English equivalent, since the quality has, unlike our twentieth century 'reason', only a superficial connection with intellect, is more subtle than 'reasonableness' and more emotional than the eighteenth century implications of the term. Perhaps we might pertinently describe Fauré's art as Greek if we had any idea what Greek music actually sounded like; but comparisons with sculpture are shifty ground to tread upon. Surprising though it may seem to those who know Fauré only by the early songs, we shall understand him more clearly if we see him in relation to Bach.

Even at the beginning of his career Fauré, a real conservative, set out, like Bach, using only those tools with which he was familiar by environment and upbringing. His æsthetic was from the start similar to Bach's, for he regarded music as, essentially, something that is *constructed*. He was a 'pure' musician, unimpressed by Debussy's emphasis on colour and hyper-tremulousness of sensibility working by way of harmonic innovation, and with no interest whatever in the 'thrilling' sonorous potentialities of the modern orchestra. [1] In the matter of variety

(1) 'Tone-colour', which was excessively exploited by the Wagner-nurtured orchestrators of his time, seemed to Fauré dangerously like a substitute for the real stuff of music, but we must not glibly assume that because he seldom composed for orchestra he was therefore unable to. His habit of leaving the instrumentation of his incidental and dramatic music to other hands makes it difficult to decide how much of the alleged Fauréan orchestration is genuine, but the few indisputable examples are enough to prove that, though his sensibility did not often call for orchestral expression, he could on occasion masterfully adapt the orchestra to his own ends. The scoring of the Requiem, for instance—so unatmospheric, level and apparently 'colourless'—is superb, sensitive and alive to the minutest detail, and almost Berliozian in its finesse and clarity.

M. Koechlin suggests further that Fauré's indifference to the orchestra was not altogether independent of economic factors; he might have written more orchestral work if he could have secured orchestras capable of performing his music sympathetically.

of figuration and pianistic device there is, except perhaps in his very last works, nothing that would have alarmed Saint-Saëns or Schumann, nor did he play any direct part in the breakdown of the old system of tonality. His rhythms are not strikingly multifarious or unexpected, he showed not a glimmer of interest in the emancipation of rhythm which was led by such figures as Stravinsky. He created for himself a medium of extraordinary fluidity and subtlety by expanding traditional methods rather than by revolting from them ; essentially, he never revoked the methods of his immediate predecessors. We can see now what prodigious strength of character his placid resistance to Wagner and Debussy and the later *arrivistes* actually meant. Even those conservative rhythms, though they have not the proud solidity—the pulse, as it were, of a great age in which time was comparatively unhurried—of the rhythms of Bach, may yet be said to imply, equally, an ordered and civilized attitude to experience.

Now Fauré transforms the emasculated academic idiom of his time (the idiom of Saint-Saëns) into an idiom of almost Bach-like potency by means of his virile sense of melodic line and his mastery of the bass. There is, literally, nothing in contemporary music that can be compared with the sheer force, the calm and ordered strength, of Fauré's later melodies. They may have 'charm'—the quality ignorantly associated with all Fauré's work—they may be sensuous sometimes, tender or melancholy, but they combine, always, massiveness with their grace, and their latent energy is immense. Consider the strong, radiant profile, free from emotional chromaticism, of the first movement of the Second Violin Sonata, or the Andante of the Second Quintet—the latter remarkable for its irrepressible *length* of line, spirally evolving and strengthening, never relaxed. This sustained *élan* and directness of line, like a pure and inexhaustible jet of water, belongs to a world comparable to the golden clarity of Bach, and Fauré's device of unharassed ornament in his melodic repetitions is a direct transference of an important facet of Bach's idiom, to his own.

As in Bach's art, too, these winged melodies soar over basses of wonderful suppleness and elasticity. Melody and bass are mutually independent, yet mutually fructifying. Nowhere is the *power* of Fauré's mature art more patent than in this solid tension between melody and bass;

delayed basses (*cf.* the Tenth Nocturne, or the songs 'Je me poserai sur ton cœur' and 'Dans le pénombre') are managed with a facility and concentration which gives even the most drab-seeming rhythms a glowing freshness and originality :

Je me po-se-rai   sur ton cœur   Com- me l'ois-eau

— sur   la   mer

This architectural solidity is modified by two features
of Fauré's technique. The first is the *incidental* rhythmic
freedom which his melodic thinking attains to—
the subtle phrase-grouping which he is able to
effect *within* a conservative rhythmic framework. This
rhythmic subtlety was undoubtedly developed through the
interaction of his delicate sympathy for the inflections of
the French language with his early study of Gregorian
chant, as we may see in almost any of his later songs :

Les gol - fes em - bau-més, les î - les im - mor-tel - les ont pour

vous,____ Cy-gne noir,____ des ré-cifs pé - ril - leux.   *etc.*

but while the supreme fruits of it are to be found
in the wonderful combination of inflectional fluidity with
structural discipline in the final songs, such as 'Mirages'
and 'Le Jardin Clos', it is I think true to say that some
such rhythmic compromise, vocally founded, is found in
almost all his mature music, instrumental work as well as
songs.

The second feature modifying his constructive solidity
is his incidental plasticity of tonality, which complements
the incidental rhythmic plasticity just referred to. With
his Gregorian training it was natural enough for Fauré
to use plagal cadences in order to avoid the 'romantic' and
emotional leading-note and to substitute the unresolved
fourth for the third in chords of the seventh and ninth,

thereby producing effects of a characteristic tranquillity. But the intrinsic nature of his modality is manifested in the way in which, gliding rapidly from one mode to another, he effects very delicate enharmonic transitions, so that one wonders whether his conception of modulation is not as close to the 'cadential' conception of the sixteenth century polyphonists as to the key-relationship system of classical European music. In the modern sense of the term, Fauré's final pieces modulate so rapidly that they can hardly be said to modulate at all; his line exists in a perpetual flux between tonality and modality, but this does not mean that it is looser than the line of classical music, only that it is more fluid and, in a paradoxical way, more rather than less highly organized. In such a passage as the following one can see that the balance between incessant 'melodic' modulation—a modulation effected by chromatic and enharmonic alteration in the component lines—and the harmonic periods on which the work is built, is always scrupulously maintained :

One will find, for instance, that the modulations are always more condensed in the development sections of sonata movements than in the expositions; the clarity of the proportions is not endangered by the incidental harmonic and tonal 'colourings', to use the seventeenth century term.

The term has, I think, a peculiar appropriateness because Fauré's technique in many ways seems to occupy a position half-way between the methods of the sixteenth century and those of the later eighteenth century, rather similar to that occupied by the seventeenth century and early eighteenth century baroque composers. His music is, as we have seen, centred in melody and bass, and the purpose of the bass is to give harmonic stability; but at the same time the bass is also, like Couperin's, linearly conceived—as a melodic part—and the concentration of the harmonies is the consequence of the flexible opposition between the two lines which form the architectural skeleton of the whole composition. Similarly, like that of the eighteenth century baroque composer, Fauré's method in his bigger chamber works is to build up movement over a regular rhythmic pulse and a consistent figuration; but the rapid enharmonic transitions of tonal centre and the manner in which the figuration lyrically *evolves*— so that the growth of figuration and the flow of the tonalities become inseparably the 'form', the architecture—are clearly allied to the technique of the sixteenth century in which melodic growth, polyphonically conceived, is composition. Perhaps Bach occupies a comparable position in relation to the sixteenth century. His choral preludes and violin and clavier sonatas for instance require a similar technique in performance to Fauré's late chamber works such as the second violin sonata, the string quartet and the two piano quintets. In all the performers must think melodically in long stretches of tone, playing in level contrasted periods of forte and piano, without emotionally expressive dynamics; in all the phrasing of the figuration and the shifts of the harmony will convey all the 'expression' that is necessary. Fauré carries incidental tonal plasticity further than do Bach and Couperin, of course; but the attitude in all of them is the same. Concentration upon lyrical gemination rather than *contrasted* thematic and tonal centres gives to their music a quasi-religious 'detachment from self', and to their texture a characteristic density and interior potency.

To sum up we might say that the *strength* of Fauré's music is synonymous with his conception of an ordered, balanced civilization, in a sense to which the conditions of the world to-day are not congenial; and this ordered civilization is manifested musically in the Bach-like characteristics of his work, his spacious structure (related to the Bach aria, more architectural and reflective, less dramatic, than the Mozart allegro), his long serene melodies and basses, his unperturbed rhythms and command of canon and counter-point. The *charm* of his music is seen to be synonymous with his apprehension of the *parfum impérissable,* a sort of culture that may with difficulty still persist in a man of the modern world; and this European grace is revealed in the delicacy of his elliptical harmonies and enharmonic transitions, a subtlety of inflection and of modulation which is often (in *Penelope* for instance) startlingly reminiscent of those aspects of Monteverdi's operatic writing, which form a transition between sixteenth century 'texture' and the idiom of the classical baroque. In both, the hyper-sensitive impression depends on the relations between chords which are in themselves usually simple enough; augmented and diminished intervals are by no means as common as the effect of poignancy might lead one, at a casual hearing, to suppose. We have established the general correspondences between the civilization his music incarnates and that of Bach and the Renaissance, respectively : if we wish to obtain a more specific notion of its nature we must turn to the consideration of particular compositions.

The early songs do not concern us here except in so far as the later manner is implicit in them. They are an extremely subtilized extension from the music of Gounod, the notorious relation to Schumann, presented in the text-book account, being, as M. Koechlin has pointed out, almost entirely illusory. The German *lied* had its roots in peasant art, the French *mélodie* is essentially artificial and, if it has any antecedents before Gounod, they are to be found in French key-board music of the seventeenth and eighteenth centuries. The *mélodie* was an art-form perfected, towards the end of the nineteenth century, as an exquisite medium for the expression of *sensibilité*, of the adolescent desires and lavendered languors of such an admirable period-piece as Chausson; or for the creation of the private world of regression—*la vie intérieure*—which came to be associated pre-eminently with Debussy. Fauré's own private world of paradisal parks and twilit balconies is surprisingly varied, ranging from the diffident, enigmatic elegance of 'Les Présents' and 'Le Secret', and the nonchalant luxury of 'Les Roses d'Ispahan', to the fervour of 'Après un Rêve' and the luminous volup-tuousness of 'Nell', while the verve and shapeliness of these melodies, the subtlety of modulation, suggests that in this private fancy-world of Fauré is the tiny life-sperm of that re-creation of ideal French civilization which is to be his mature art.

The first composition in which this re-creation is indubitably effected seems to me to be the Requiem Mass op. 48 (1887). Here subtilized Gounod has become an idiom as individual, as potent, as that of Bach, though its range is, of course, slighter. Fauré calls for only a small orchestra and chorus and never once, not even at the climaxes, dis-turbs the tranquil flow of the music in which the harmonies are undemonstrative and the melodic construction of almost Mozartian simplicity; yet few compositions of to-day give so powerful an impression of grandeur and nobility. Con-sider the bell-clear repose of the beautiful tune to which 'Te decet' is sung, the finely moulded 'Hostias et preces' with its background of evanescent, fluctuating harmonies, the simple line of the 'Pie Jesus', the poised melody of the 'Tremens factus' with its gently grim pizzicato accompaniment. Here is no accent of fear, no sarcasm, no grotesquerie 'no external effect (to quote Nadia Boulanger) detracts from its sober and somewhat severe expression of grief ; no disquiet or agitation disturbs its profound meditation, no doubt tarnishes its unassailable faith, its quiet confidence, its tender and peaceful expectation . . . a sorrow so near to God that it is without revolt, cry or gesture'. As M. Koechlin has remarked, it is difficult to find any music, since the great composers of the Roman Church and the chorales of Bach, as externally grave and simple, with such internal stress and fire.

The Requiem gives us Fauré the exquisite, the elegant, in whom exquisiteness is linked with austerity. For the authentic Fauréan *power* we have to wait until the superb song cycle *La Bonne Chanson* (Verlaine), op. 61, the Sixth and Seventh Piano Nocturnes op. 63 and op. 74, and the dramatic work *Promethée,* op. 83. This is music of intense lyrical passion, with much greater abundance of detail though firmly and spaciously constructed—music resplendent in *Promethée,* sultry and ecstatic in the piano pieces, in the song cycle of almost delirious joyfulness and candour.

In the works of the final years—the compositions to which my account of Fauré's technique principally applies —a complete synthesis is achieved between these modes of exquisite austerity and joyous strength. These works include the song cycles *La Chanson d'Eve* (op. 95), *Le Jardin Clos* (op. 106), *Mirages* (op. 113), and *L'Horizon Chimérique* (op. 118) ; the Piano Trio, the Second Quintet, the Second Violin Sonata, the String Quartet, the piano Preludes and the later Nocturnes and Barcarolles. Here, with such a song as 'Inscription sur le sable' or 'Danseuse', Fauré wonderfully evokes the infinite and eternal, rooted in the human and humane, through the medium of his austere arias and shifting harmonies. The gravity and lyricism, the ardour and reticence, the tormented energy and philosophic serenity, are ever more inextricably interlinked. The radiance of the first movement of the Second Quintet; the bounding naïveté, the pure *premier matin du monde* atmosphere—perhaps related to the candour of the French nursery song—of the finale of the Second Violin Sonata; the sad dignity of *L'Horizon Chimérique;* all these are ostensibly of the same world, a world in which things are visualized in bright daylight, unclouded by the mists of imagined profundities. There are real profundities beneath the *élan* of theme and structure; but even the undertones are sunlit.

In the very last works, perhaps, the radiance diminishes. There is a strange descending mournfulness in the mirror-like stillness and undulating figurations of the incomparable 'Danseuse', in the gravely shaped lines, the curious scales and flexing nuances of that beautiful funeral oration the Eleventh Nocturne, in the glassy four-part writing of the Thirteenth Nocturne and of the String Quartet—a funeral accent which is new to Fauré's music :

This is a sombre art, stark and impersonal, yet containing an infinite lugubriousness and lassitude. In the fluttering harmonies of the last Barcarolle (No. 13) there is even a suggestion of twilight, of something tremulous and phantasmogoric, like a scene viewed between sleeping and waking—a phenomenon very odd in a music habitually so maturely civilized, so effulgent with daylight clarity.

And I think we can understand how this should be so if we remember that Fauré is the *consummation* of French civilization, that he did not appear until those native qualities of sensibility which had made French civilization what it was, and had made Fauré's ideal civilization possible, were, if not on the point of dispersal, at least becoming tarnished by extraneous influences. So that, although Fauré's music represents a victory of civilization, it is also at the same time an elegy, and I suspect that the composer was aware of this, emotionally if not intellectually, at the time when he wrote his final works ; his music has the ripeness, the gloss, of an autumnal fruit. In this connection Fauré's work bears a resemblance to the poetry of another great conservative, Paul Valéry. The luminous images and shifting undertones of rhythm of 'Cimetière Marin' have the same atmosphere as the clear lines and the bitter-sweet harmonic quiverings, of Fauré's music, and it is possible that Fauré occupies in the history of French music a position analogous to that occupied by Valéry in the history of French literature. Both are artists of civilization, guardians of tradition, and, in a sense, artists of the elegiac. 'Density' and 'interior potency' are terms applicable to the technique of both poet and composer. The correspondences are, of course, vague and general, but I think they are worth noticing.

The comparison with Valéry suggests other reasons for the hostility, or indifference, of the general public to Fauré's art. *Je dois compter vingt ans pour qu'une de mes œuvres soit apprécié du public* he said, and accepted this state of affairs with diffident resignation. Because he creates an organized vision or an objectified body of experience, as it were out of himself, he is a difficult composer to listen to. It is necessary to listen to him attentively for, like Valéry, he disdains facility, and the surface effect. His idiom, so consummately constructed, yields its full flavour only with familiarity, and it is so subtle and reticent an idiom that it is likely to repel those who have not a certain measure of general cultivation. His mature work, with the possible exception of the mondain, but elegantly distinguished, Valses Caprices, is uniformly serious and pure in style, making no concession to the fancy or cruder emotional responses; his indifference to the public fortunes of his music, his disregard of public opinion, is difficult to parallel in an age in which composers seek consolation for their lack of popular appreciation in the formation of cliques and the cultivation of a pert smart-alecism.

Yet we are beginning to respond to this proudly idealistic art. We see now, I think, that Fauré's art is probably, with that of that very different composer Debussy, the most important thing that has happened in French music since Berlioz, and one of the few 'imperishable' monuments of his time. He shows us, in the ordered bodying forth of experience which is his music, a civilization not quite of our time, stronger and calmer than our time and for that reason immensely valuable for us. *L'artiste doit aimer la vie et nous montrer qu'elle est belle. Sans lui, nous en douterions.* Fauré himself made this simple, if pretentious, claim for his art, and he would have wished no greater satisfaction than to know that we are coming to believe that his music falls but little short of his promise. There is not much music altogether, and almost no contemporary music at all, for which a similar claim could be substantiated.

And Fauré's music—of this there is no doubt—can never become dated. He taught us that construction, as Baudelaire said, is the one and only sure guarantee of the mysterious life of the workings of the mind.

Fauré died over fifteen years ago. Unrecognized for so long, his work should to-day be studied by any conscientious musician, and his relevance, his importance, is likely to increase in the near future. Yet the values he stood for, immensely important in themselves, have no longer quite the same significance or the same urgency, 'civilization' becomes at once a more complicated and a less subtle ideal. A composer the native mould of whose sensibility was similar to Fauré's, would write, to-day, music *essentially* different from Fauré's; he would write, I think, music rather like that of Albert Roussel.

Scrutiny 1938 (Revised 1945).

IV

ALBERT ROUSSEL AND LA MUSIQUE FRANÇAISE

'. . . le culte des valeurs spirituelles est à la base de
toute société qui se prétend civilisée et la musique, parmi
les arts, en est l'expression la plus sensible et la plus
élevée.'   —ALBERT ROUSSEL.

I

ONE WOULD NOT SAY that Roussel is ever likely to
be a popular composer, but his career is, among contemporary musicians, almost unique in that he has been
treated, even when misunderstood, with the respect that
ought, in any civilized society, to accrue to the serious artist.
He came to music late; he proved himself consummate
master of the materials of his craft; he was recognized as a
personality whom it was impossible not to respect. Young
musicians have looked to him as a contemporary, but a
contemporary whose experience and wisdom their
inexperience might envy and admire; older musicians
admitted that they could not understand him but knew
they had no right to smile. They did not smile; and even
the most recalcitrant were in the long run converted. His
reputation was, and is, international, unlike Fauré's, for
the latter was accepted only in his own country. He dedicated himself to his art as religiously as did Fauré, but he
makes contact with the life of to-day at more points and
in more ways, for Fauré's conception of civilization
belongs, as I have shown, in a sense to the past. It may be
that this explains why discerning musicians of all countries
have respected Roussel as the French respected Fauré—
even the pugnacious Mr. Sorabji, who can hardly be suspected of a temperamental partiality for French music,
saluted the later symphonies as music with heart and guts

—at last a juicy steak amid the perpetual bubble and
squeak of present-day music-making. We respect Roussel's
integrity, his eager love of his art; and we feel that he
too has had to grapple with the problems that confront
us. We are on more comfortable ground with Roussel than
in tackling Fauré who remained so majestically aloof from
many of the values we are forced to live by. But perhaps
Roussel might be called a more difficult composer in the
sense that he is more sophisticated.

Here, anyway, is something to start from. I suggested
in the postscript to my Fauré essay that Roussel's music
was the sort of music that a man with a sensibility similar
to that of Fauré might write if he were confronted with
the problems of the modern world. One could make the
point more neatly by suggesting that whereas Fauré is
civilized, Roussel is urbane. I do not use the word pejora-
tively, for his urbanity represents always a serious and
sometimes even a solemn attitude to life; but I do want it
to suggest Roussel's greater self-consciousness, his peculiar
modernity. We recognize Fauré as being aristocratic,
'polished'; but his polish is inseparable from, indeed is,
his civilization. We recognize Roussel as polished also, but
by calling him urbane we imply that the relation between
his civilization, his sophistication and his way of ordering
his experience is complex and precarious as Fauré's conception of civilization had no need to be. He is the more
self-conscious, the more allusive in his cultivation. I do not
want to suggest that either attitude is superior to the other.
But I do think that to insist on this distinction between
Roussel's *urbanity* and Fauré's *civilization* is a key to an
intelligent approach to Roussel's music. If the distinction
seems at the moment hazy, my apology must be that to
elucidate it is what I am trying to do in this essay.

II

As far as concerns the earliest works the distinction is
pretty obviously and simply pertinent. The point is often
made that they are written in an idiom which is a com-

promise between d'Indy and Debussy—on the one hand 'formal', on the other impressionistic—though the somewhat Parsifalish ascetic aspects of d'Indy's music can hardly have been congenial to Roussel. These works are, anyway, though intensely French, rather naïvely sophisticate in their subtle inflexion of line, almost a superior sort of dilettante music, the same *type* of music as Ravel was writing at the time, though cruder and less accomplished. The first piano pieces, the *Rustiques* (1904)—I pass over the initial amateurish exercise, *Des Heures Passent* (1898) —the first symphony, *Poème de la Forêt* (1905), the first Trio (1902) and the first Violin Sonata (1907), all these are overlong and meandering but none is without distinction. The reconciliation of impressionism with 'classical' formalism is the achievement of a personality of real force and originality, not merely a facile if intelligent tampering with other composers' mannerisms. To describe the technique of d'Indy and of impressionism is unnecessary; it is familiar enough, can be easily investigated at first hand, and anyway has little bearing on the work of Roussel's maturity. What I want to do here is to indicate briefly characteristics in these earliest compositions which are Roussel's own, which make his use of the d'Indy-Debussy technique inimitable. They are all traits which will be developed in the Rousselian technique of maturity, a technique which cannot be properly understood unless it is realized that the germ of it is present in the earliest compositions.

Firstly, both the melodic and rhythmic structures of these works bears some relation to the traditional French *chanson;* the tunes have a racy vigour that reminds us that Roussel knew and admired the *beau musicien de la campagne* Déodat de Séverac, but at the same time he is never, like de Séverac, simply a regional composer. It is not merely that he uses basically, the impressionistic, arty, technique ; so did de Séverac. But his attitude to his rusticity is not simple but extremely sophisticated ; if his melodies have qualities resembling those of the *chanson,* they wear them with an air of deliberate decorativeness and whimsicality. Roussel sometimes assumes an air of wide-eyed bumpkin innocence; but he does not let us forget that he is at heart the sophisticated man of cultivation—I almost said 'man of the world'—who writes those impressionistic harmonies, and the charm of his early music comes largely from this placing together, in melodic and harmonic structure, of two apparently opposed points of view.

Roussel's rusticity is, then, in these early works, partly artificial. One might bring out the nature of this artificiality by suggesting that if his tunes are reminiscent of those of the *chanson,* it is the *chanson* in an eighteenth century setting that he is most interested in. Even at this date, though he takes over in some measure the prevailing technique of .Debussy, the seeds of the revolt against impressionism are sown. Like de Séverac's, his early music is, of course, in a sense music of the open air and of the sun—the *Poème de la Forêt* is even directly evocative and illustrative. But he is much more equivocal than de Séverac in trying to create a musical corollary for the ecstasies of sea and sunlight; nor is he ever, like Debussy, interested in sensation for its own sake. The *Poème de la Forêt* may be a successful piece of nature music; but what we are most conscious of is not its evocative brilliance but its geniality of melody, the precision and ingenuity of its rhythmic structure, its exquisite placing of sonorities and timbres. The *Divertissement* for wind instruments (1906) reveals explicitly what we had always suspected; that it is not so much the 'natural' aspects of Nature that appeal to Roussel as the eighteenth century elements of *champêtre* and *fête galante*. The *Divertissement* is a musical evocation of the eighteenth century *parc* of rivers, woods and lawns, a world of the *fantasque à la* Watteau, such as Debussy was more bitterly to turn to in his last years. The tunes are slender, but have an unimpeded dulcet lyricism, a delicious pastoral suavity, an autumnal gentleness and melancholy gentility; the rhythms are elaborate, yet tactfully controlled. With its rhythmic ingenuity, the

neat solidity of its lines, the unexpected placing of
its harmonies, the *Divertissement* was in its way as important an event in musical history as Stravinsky's *Sacre*.
Roussel had, in 1906, done with real melodic distinction
what Poulenc was to do with less vigour and originality
fifteen or twenty years later. We shall see later how this
elegant artificiality becomes not altogether distinct from
the Tradition of the *Commedia dell' Arte*.

In describing these early works we have concentrated
mainly on their relation to French music of the past as
revealed in their melodic and rhythmic structure. But there
is one harmonic peculiarity which immediately distin-
guishes his work from that of any other composer of the
time using the same more or less Debussyan idiom, and
that is his use of the tritone. The central position given
by Roussel to the tritone in his harmonic scheme is so
characteristic that it might almost be called a mannerism.
It is noticeable in his very earliest compositions and helps
to give that oddly acrid quality to their bucolic sophistication. The device may be part of his legacy from
d'Indy who got it, of course, from Wagner; but there is
little resemblance between d'Indy's use of the tritone and
Roussel's; in d'Indy it has a rather emasculating effect
while it is one of the conditions of Roussel's caustic vigour.

All these qualities are developed and synthesized in the
first compositions of Roussel's maturity, the piano Suite
op. 14 (1911), the piano Sonatina op. 16 (1912), the ballet
Le Festin d'Araignée op. 17 (1912), and a few songs. These
works may be called mature in the sense that in them the
rather jejune *ambivalence* between the bucolic and the
sophisticated is first resolved into what for want of a better
word we must call an 'attitude'—a way of experiencing
which is *at once* toughly earthy and hyperfastidious and
cultivated. In technical terms one can make the same
point by saying that the idiom no longer depends on art-
fully *juxtaposing* the idiosyncracies of impressionism with
those of, say, the *chanson* and the eighteenth century, but

evolves 'from within', is a dialect peculiar to Roussel and to
no one else. The Suite is composed of traditional French
dance forms treated with the sardonic brilliance characteristic of Roussel. Except in the tender, elegant, and
Watteau-like Sicilienne the music is brusque and racy, of
a bucolic toughness but with a fine alacrity and distinction in the contour of the lines. The Sonatina manifests a
trenchancy almost Haydnesque, with a brittle Scherzo
such as we shall become familiar with in the later works,
an adagio with a robust if dolorous melody in a swaying
irregular measure, and a finale (telescoped with the
adagio) in complex rhythmic formation—a movement as
sunlit as de Séverac, but much more sinewy and ironic.
Le Festin, the best known, I suppose, of all Roussel's
works, is pastoral music in essence, music of the most witty
and genial lyricism of spirit; and it gains its flavour from
what might almost be called a harmonic system developed
from syncopated fourths and tritones.

The rhythms of these works, supple and undulating, for
the most part based on traditional French dance forms
yet so briskly unexpected, testify to a sense of *physical
movement* that no modern composer can rival. Some of
the songs employ modern dance forms with the same
éclat; *Amoureux Séparés,* written, surprisingly, in 1906, is
a tango of delicate but full-blooded suavity.

III

ROUSSEL, marin favorisé,
Entrelacant l'ancre à la lyre,
Les moussons et les alisés
Servent le gré de ton navire . . .

Before he decided on a musical career at the age of
twenty-five, Roussel had, it is well known, been destined
for the sea. His love of the sea and of travel never left
him, and in 1909 he went on a long voyage to India and
the Orient. This expedition proved a turning point in his
musical life. On his travels he heard oriental music and

watched oriental dances. When he returned to France he spent a year or so maturing his impressions, then he produced his first two major compositions, the *Evocations* op. 15 (1910-11) and *Padmavati* (1914).[1]

Evocations is an odd work, a *tour de force*. It is quite deliberately an evocation of the Orient in a western technique, and hindoo and pentatonic scales are woven into a gorgeous orchestral fabric. There is, of course, no attempt to create 'atmosphere'; it is Roussel's sympathetic comment, in his own language, on the peoples and countries of the East—and we must remember that even in his earliest work Roussel had given evidence of a certain exoticism of imagination. Here is music of a strange voluptuous fascination, a rich and sumptuous power. Mr. Sorabji, who should know, places it among the few convincing evocations of the Orient in western music.

In *Padmavati* the process is carried a step further. Here there is no attempt to 'evoke' the Orient. Eastern scales and rhythms have been assimilated into the Roussel idiom, becoming as much French as oriental. Before *Padmavati* he had, of course, created his own idiom by means of the tritonal elaboration of his harmony; but it was an idiom too restricted to express anything more than the limited states of feeling I have tried to describe. After *Padmavati* he never looked back, he was done with impressionism and with all contemporary experimentism. He had added a language to the history of music, a language of powerful austerity and ardent lyricism. *Padmavati* was frowned upon by critics because of its wilful gaucherie and harmonic incompetence. Actually its technique marks a newly won vitality, and Roussel himself realized this when he wrote, in April, 1916; 'Je réfléchissais à cela hier et je me demandais justement si je n'avais pas à craindre ce nouvel état d'esprit, qui résultera de la crise actuelle, pour *Pad-*

(1) Chronologically the piano Sonatina and *Le Festin* were written *after* the *Evocations*. I regard them, however, as the consummation of the early manner not as the beginning of something new.

mavati qui a été conçue et composée entièrement avant la
guerre. Teute réflexion faite, je ne crois pas. Je ne vois
dans mon œuvre aucune trace d'influences morbides ou
deliquescentes. Il me semble au contraire que le ton general
en est plutôt viril et fort . . .' This seems to be the place
to give some account of this fresh technical mastery—
of the typical late Roussel language in which all the works
after *Padmavati* were with various modifications to be
written.

IV

In one important respect Roussel's technique resembles
that of Fauré—in that he generally works, particularly in
his mature compositions, not by a process of 'thematic
development' (in Beethoven's sense) but by a process of
lyrical germination. Fauré achieves in his last works such
as the second violin sonata a balance between lyrical evolution and harmonic architecture which makes it not
inapposite to compare him to Couperin and Bach;
Roussel's technique does not attain to so clearly defined
an autocracy but embraces the whole range of the French
tradition; his relation to the past is both more comprehensive and more self-conscious.

Essentially he thinks lyrically and vocally rather than
instrumentally; but he strains the 'natural' conventions
of lyricism to their furthest point. His lines tend to be
enormously long and flexible in rhythm, and although,
like those of mediaeval composers, they have usually a
vocal basis, they are not confined to any one modal or
diatonic convention. They are rendered more sinewy and
intense through the prevalent use of augmented seconds
and fourths and through continual oscillations round a
fixed point as in Asiatic musics; more suave and fluid by
the pentatonic figures of Chinese (and most folk-) music.
The characteristics of eastern music and mediaeval music
—the complex rhythms, the undulating flow—are
absorbed into a personal melodic sense which establishes

its own order within a multiplicity of modalisms :

His melodic method is similar to Fauré's ; but the range of modal formulæ which he permits himself is much wider. I hope it is not necessary to point out that width is not necessarily 'progress'.

Moreover not only is his music modally kaleidoscopic in its line ; but each component line is so independently of the others. The subtlety and concentration of the harmony in his late work is due mostly to the manner in which the lines creating the polyphonic structure are not only continually shifting their tonal centre, but do not necessarily modulate simultaneously in the same direction :

and

F

Continual 'unorthodox' modifications of the tetrachord are thereby produced, which are often intensified by interior pedals and unresolved appoggiaturas. Such poly-modal thinking is both more subtle and more natural than strict polytonality in which different keys of the same diatonic system are employed at once.

Fauré, like Bach, lives half-way between polyphonic and homophonic thought. Roussel essentially thinks in polyphonic terms, as is inevitable if his polymodal con-ception of line is to attain free expression. It follows that his music depends much less than Fauré's on tension between melody and bass : with him all the parts tend to be of equal significance, and the convention of the 'harmonic' bass is alien to his idiom. It is noteworthy that his most recognizable harmonic mannerisms—such as the use of the tritone, the major seventh, and the chord of the eleventh with the seventh sharpened—are the result of certain peculiarities of his melodic-polyphonic thinking, rather than harmonic traits in their own right. In such a passage as the following :

we can see an extreme instance of the truth that it is

the way a composer *uses* chords—the context they appear
in—that is interesting. Roussel's basses have an importance
equal to but by no means greater than that of his middle
parts, whether it be in such diverse manifestations of his
genius as the austere chromaticism of the *March Funèbre*
from *Padmavati,* the comparative diatonicism of the
chorales and fugues of the *Psaume,* or the supple canonic
writing of the Piano Concerto.

Rhythmically the Roussel language is rich and complex,
inevitably so since his melody and polyphony are rich and
complex. But he preserves, as we shall see, his respect for
the traditional dance forms of France and of eighteenth
century Europe. His rhythmic vitality and sanity perhaps
comes from this compromise between freedom and discipline. Roussel's æsthetic, in so far as he can be said to
have had one, was very simple :

'Ce que je voudrais réaliser, c'est une musique se satis-
faisant à elle-même, une musique qui cherche à
s'affranchir de tout élément pittoresque et descriptif et à
jamais éloignée de toute localisation dans l'espace . . . Loin
de vouloir décrire je m'efforce toujours d'écarter de mon
esprit le souvenir des objets et des formes susceptibles de
se traduire en effets musicaux. Je ne veux faire que la
musique'.

There are to be no more 'evocations'.

V

Padmavati is one of the major achievements of the
twentieth century ; but it is in Roussel's development a
transitional work. Without knowledge of it it is difficult
to understand the works in the late manner and perhaps
the reason why *Pour un Fête du Printemps* and the
Second Symphony appeared at first so baffling was that
they were actually performed before *Padmavati,* presen-
tation of which was delayed, owing to the war and
consequent economic difficulties, until 1925. After *Padmavati* Roussel never again touched, except indirectly, on

exotic subjects; but he had learned from oriental music the direction which his melodic thinking was to take. The language he evolved for *Pour un Fête* and for the Second Symphony—the language I have tried to describe in the preceding section—remained his musical speech for the rest of his career. He modified and simplified it; but it remained substantially the same.

One might make the point more concretely by suggesting that hearing the modal melodies, the subtle inflexions and complex rhythmic organization of oriental music awoke Roussel to a realization of the true nature of his own heritage. The relation of his earliest music to the *chanson* tends to be, as I have shown, decorative and whimsical; the first mature pieces express a serious attitude, but are still somewhat topically sophisticate in their urbanity and locally regional in their rurality. In the late works he has realized, whether consciously or not, that he, born at Tourçoing, in French Flanders, belongs to the tradition that produced the great religious and troubadour composers, the tradition of Perotin, Machaut, Binchois, Dufay and Jannequin. Of course his music only superficially 'resembles' theirs; he has not their European culture. But this is what his new-found rhythmic and melodic independence—his sanity, his suppleness, the mature humour or melancholy of his linear inflexions—really means; he has divested the idiosyncrasies of his earlier work of their merely topical and local elements, he has taken his place in the evolving tradition of *la musique française*. Certainly there is not much contemporary music which has this poise and ripeness of attitude. The late works of Vaughan Williams have something of the same toughness, and perhaps Vaughan Williams' relation to the tradition of English music is similar to that of Roussel to Machaut and Jannequin; but the idiom of Vaughan Williams is hardly one that can be called urbane. Against this, one must admit that the nobly civilized music of Vaughan Williams' Fifth Symphony is probably a more remarkable achieve-

ment than Roussel's, considering the provinciality of the
contemporary English musical background compared with
the French.

There is one more aspect of this relation, in the last
works, to the traditional *chanson* to be noticed. On the
one hand the relation to the *chanson* provides a link
between Roussel and fifteenth century French music and
the work of the Flemish polyphonists; on the other hand
it connects him, by way of the nursery song, with the
tunes of the café-concert and hence with certain aspects
of the art of Erik Satie. The poise of his best work
is to be attributed to the equilibrium he achieves between
these various ways of feeling—the Latin culture he
inherits from France (partly a mature Machaut-like
lyricism, partly sympathy with the French eighteenth
century classical forms); the robust gravity and
impudent drolerie he inherits from Flanders (*cf.* the
enormous melodies of his adagios, and some of the tunes
of the scherzi); and the equivocal naïveté and sophisticated brutality he shares with the French nursery song and
the tune of the café-concert, respectively (*cf.* the relation
of the scherzi to Chabrier, Bizet and Satie). The
rhythmic poise which I have noticed earlier as being produced by a combination of melodic freedom with the
discipline of the movements of the dance is, of course,
a more particular example of the same maturity of
attitude. We can understand what Roussel meant when he
said that he hated 'tout sentiment résultant d'une hyper-
trophie du *moi*'. We shall be examining further these
various traits in considering with some particularity the
works in the final, the 'classical', manner.

VI

Roussel was aware, himself, that *Pour un Fête* and the
Second Symphony (op. 22 and 23, respectively, composed
1919-21), marked a fresh stage in his musical career.

'Je travaillerai' (he writes), 'avec plus d'ardeur et de frénésie que jamais. Jamais je ne suis senti aussi dispos et aussi frais d'esprit et aussi dégagé de toute influence, et cela provient évidemment du grand repos de mon cerveau . . .' The new polymodal technique, the harmonic system of appogiaturas is in these works consummated; the task of simplification—of concentration—remains. In 1925 Roussel retired to Vasterival, a small fishing village congenial to his temperament, and in one year produced *La Naissance de la Lyre* op. 24, the Sérénade for flute, violin, viola, cello and harp, op. 30, the second Violin Sonata, op. 28, the Suite in F, op. 33, and a number of songs. These works inaugurate the 'new classicism' of the final manner.

The manner is called 'classical' because it represents a return to *le style continu*, compared with the fragmentary methods of the impressionists. In *La Naissance de la Lyre* and the Sérénade the lyricism is more supple, the harmony more acid, the orchestration delicate and fluid. The Suite is written in three eighteenth century dance forms; a Prelude with a fierce, jaunty rhythmic pulse and an immense bounding second subject characterized by abrupt leaps and racy twists; a Sarabande with a long flowing line of a sweet yet powerful elegance and sumptiousness of stature[2]; and a Gigue in which a comic truculent nursery tune is introduced on the trumpet, the entry being timed with consummate skill so that the balance between the ludicrously vulgar (the café-chantant element) and the vigorously earthy (the folk-tune element) is perfectly poised. It is movements like this that remind one of Satie,

(2) I use the word stature in an attempt to indicate the curiously static quality of the Sarabande and some other of Roussel's late slow movements—a sense of motion within immobility. The rhythmic feeling is subtle and strong but it seems, as it were, disembodied. It is rather like an aural form of the visual phenomenon of watching a cinematograph representation of a slow and courtly dance (which the Sarabande is); one applauds and appraises the elegance of the pose, the charm of the movement, while remaining personally aloof.

not only in their chanson-like lilt and persistent repetition of rhythmic formulæ, but also in that urbane distinction and precariousness in the melodic contour[3]—a subtle, almost cynical detachment (note the caustic insouciance given to the nursery tune by flattening the leading note). His instrumentation is unatmospheric, taut, but with a knack of juxtaposing sharply defined sonorities for the sake of polyphonic clarity, which helps to give his music its stringent, almost wry flavour.

'J'ai toujours poursuivi le dessin de la construction et du rhythme ; le récherche de la forme et du développement ont été ma constante préoccupation.' This sentence of Roussel emphasizes his concern for discipline in these compositions of his final years. The setting of Psalm LXXX uses only the simplest technical means, so simple as to appear on paper almost gauche ; yet it attains in its detached way—for Roussel's urbanity hardly presupposes any accepted religious creed—to a farouche majesty and grandeur. The *Concert* for small orchestra, op. 34 (1927) and the *Petite Suite*—Aubade, Pastorale, and Mascarade, op. 39 (1929) have a sprightly concision that makes them the music *par excellence* of the *Commedia dell' Arte;* and the Piano Concerto, op. 36 (1927), with its percussive rhythms and bouncing themes in the first movement, its comic frustrated café-chantant tune in the finale—we may compare some of the tunes of Wiéner, though Roussel's tunes are much less 'juicy', more aristocratically poised—attains in the adagio to a truly noble chastity of line and distinction of pianistic ornament.

A peak point of the Rousselian idiom is reached in the Third Symphony (1930). All the elements we have noticed combine here with deeper substance and

(3) I know Satie's melodies are short and symmetrical whereas Roussel's are longish and complex; that is the inevitable reflection of the simple single-mindedness of Satie's sensibility and the comparative tortuosity of Roussel's. But the fact that Satie is so miraculously single-minded also means that he is a much smaller and more limited composer than Roussel.

richness. The first movement has the familiar prancing modally inflected themes, the ferocious pulsing rhythmic organization—the sense of physical movement. The ripe adagio reaches a climax in a clattering fugue and then subsides serenely in a soaring aria for violin. The Scherzo is a racy waltz, more acrid version of Chabrier; the finale combines a chanson-like lyricism with passages of tranquil melodic solemnity. The Fourth Symphony (1934) explores similar reaches of experience but is, I think, inferior to the Third.

It is not necessary to describe the long list of compositions written, mostly at Vasterival, during the nineteen-thirties. They manifest—through the Sinfonietta, the String Trio, the Quartet and the ballets, down to the last unfinished Trio for wind instruments—no falling off from mastery and an ever more stringent economy. Perhaps the best introduction to Roussel's late work is by way of the songs of these final years. 'Cœur en Péril', elliptical but comparatively diatonic in line, offers a characteristically wry transformation of the clichés of Spanish music, just as the odd 'Jazz dans la Nuit', op. 38 had metamorphosed the rhythms of jazz into something as unlike jazz as it is like Roussel. 'L'Heure du Rétour' is a mournful and bitterly *fauve* perversion of the nostalgic song of the café-concert; and the two songs that comprise op. 55, 'Vieilles Cartes' and 'Si quelquefois tu pleures' are perfect examples of the Rousselian whimsical yet melancholy urbanity in their 'modally' evolving yet symmetrically poised polyphonic contour, and their consequent piquancy of harmony. In the *Deux Poèmes Chinois,* op. 47, the apparent inconsequentiality of the various linear strands—their apparent disjointedness and independence of one another—produces an effect at once amused and nonchalant, yet hardly cynical. The inconsequentiality is the result of the peculiarly French aloofness of attitude; it creates no feeling of vapidity but rather of calculated understatement.

The masterpiece of all these late songs is undoubtedly, however, 'Le Kérioklepte', from op. 44, in which the droll tune is so delicately moulded that the most simple triad or the most undemonstrative rhythm takes on, beneath it, an inexhaustibly surprising irony :

It would never have been written, obviously, but for such things of Satie as the *Ludions* and the *Quatre Petites Mélodies*—it is a case here of the pupil teaching the master; but Satie achieved nothing as profoundly human in its urbanity.

The *Rapsodie Flamande,* op. 56 (1936) might be mentioned in conclusion because it is the only occasion on which Roussel directly employs Flemish folk tunes. It is light music of delicious buoyancy, orchestrated with that crisp pungency I have already referred to. There is a berceuse transparently harmonized for strings ; the other tunes are treated with unashamedly rowdy jocularity. Again the orchestration, particularly in its use of the brass, is reminiscent of Satie. This brilliantly urbane little work should be a lesson to all sentimentally rustic folk-mongering musicians.

VII

Something remains to be said about Roussel's conception
of the place of music in opera and ballet. An account of
the history of opera might be given in terms of its tendency
to aspire now to the dramatic and realistic, now to the
balletistic ideal, and Roussel follows Satie and most twentieth century musicians in coming out, roughly speaking,
on the side of the ballet. His principles were indicated in
a programme note to *Padmavati,* with which work he said
he was trying to revive the form of opera-ballet in the
manner of Rameau :

> L'opéra-ballet se distingue de l'opéra ordinaire en
> çe que la danse y tient autant de place que le chant et
> qu'au lieu de n'intervenir que comme un divertissement
> elle doit se rattacher constamment à l'action.

Since 'tout est conventionel au théâtre' realism is a false
ideal ; the essential relation is that between music and
physical movement.

It will readily be perceived that Roussel, with his superb
musical sense of physical movement, especially as reflected
in the traditional French dance forms, combined at the
same time with his sustained melodic power and linear
freedom, was finely endowed for the creation of works
in this form, and the ballets he wrote at Vasterival,
Bacchus et Ariane (1930) and *Aenéas* (1934)—*ballet avec
chœurs*—are certainly among his most impressive accom-
plishments. He possibly learned something from Satie,
learned how to combine the maximum of personality with
the 'objective' organization of rhythmic sequences ; but
the idiom is his own, substantially that of the Concerto
for cello, op. 57 (1936), the late songs and the other works
of the period ; and it is a logical extension of principles
implicit in all his mature music. Readers wishing to
examine his method cannot do better than to read over
the extremely beautiful *Danse de Didon* and the majestic
and rhythmically exciting *Hymne Final* from *Aenéas.*

The year before he died, Roussel unexpectedly produced an opéra bouffe, *Le Testament de la Tante Caroline* (1936). I have been unable to obtain a score of this work, which seems to be unpublished. It must surely be a creation of remarkable interest—the *Rapsodie Flamande,* composed about the same time, is suggestive of the kind of fluent ironic gaiety we might expect from it, though it would probably be too allusive to be really popular.

VIII

> Un artiste dérive toujours de quelqu'un, d'un maître antérieur dont il s'est inspiré, consciemment ou inconsciemment . . . On se juge très mal soi-même et je n'arrive pas à rétrouver mon père musical . . . à qui me rattachez-vous?   —ALBERT ROUSSEL.

Roussel's distinction, I hope I have made it clear, lies in his creation of a personal language; and he has created that language because he has been aware of his place in the traditional evolution of French music; so that an attempt to estimate his position has amounted to an attempt to answer the question he asks in the quotation at the head of this section. But when I say that he is 'aware' of his position I do not mean that he has thought about it as I have tried to do in these pages; only that he has, through a long process of evolution, assimilated what he wanted from French music of the past and taken his place in the succession of figures that make up that tradition. He does not re-create in music, like Machaut, a European civilization; nor, like Couperin, a great but comparatively local French civilization; he does not express an ideally formulated civilization like Fauré. But his response to the world is that of a man who has understood and sympathized with all that Machaut and Couperin and Fauré have stood for. True, though his music is powerful, it has not the effortless power of Fauré's finest work. Yet his urbanity must, I think, for its traditional originality, be recognized as a sort of wisdom; and I suppose, anyway, that France is about the only country

that still offers the material—the cultural heritage—
necessary for such an undertaking.

I think it is significant that though his language was
universally recognized as an accomplishment independent
of, and comparable in importance with, the various revo-
lutions of the most influential of modern composers—
Stravinsky, Schönberg and Hindemith—this language has
had no influence on practising musicians ; and this despite
the fact that young composers looked to him, as a commanding personality, for guidance. (Satie took a course
of strict counterpoint under Roussel, but if there is any
question of influence involved here it is, as I have
suggested, the pupil who influenced the master. And it is
not as surprising as it superficially appears that the
Parisian-American, anti-traditional revolutionary Edgar
Varèse, should have been among Roussel's pupils.) In his
way, Roussel was as lonely a figure in his generation as
any of the less traditionally 'civilized' composers. He did
not seem to mind being lonely :

> Il n'est pas nécessaire qu'une symphonie ou un
> drame deviennent aussi populaires qu'une chanson
> de Mayol. La Musique est l'art le plus fermé et le
> plus inaccessible. C'est du musicien bien plus encore
> que du poète qu'on peut dire qu'il est complètement
> isolé dans le monde, seul avec son langage plus ou
> moins incompréhensible . . . A part deux ou trois
> belles œuvres qu'on pourrait écrire pour le peuple,
> pour des fêtes analogues aux fêtes suisses et qui
> seraient comme de grandes fresques largement
> brossées, tout le reste, dans l'état réciproque actuel
> de la musique et de la foule, sera toujours destiné
> à de très rares auditeurs.

I suppose this is sensible enough ; only it is a bit hard on
the composer who has not his genius, and his self-
sufficiency. There must be few who have the right to feel
so confident.

Scrutiny 1938 (revised 1945).

V

CHARLES KOECHLIN

'La génie musicale de la France, c'est quelque chose
comme la fantaisie dans la sensibilité.'
—CLAUDE DEBUSSY.

ALMOST ALL THE IMPORTANT figures in contemporary music have at some time in their careers been
dubbed as solitaries, and their isolation is understandable
enough : yet the positions of Sibelius, Delius, Roussel and
Bloch—to make the more obvious choices—are now secure,
and the tardiness of their acceptance came not so much
from the remoteness and difficulty of their ways of
experience (with the exception perhaps of Sibelius's Fourth
Symphony) as from the by now notorious apathy of the
musical public. The solitariness of Charles Koechlin in
the present day musical world seems, on the other hand,
to be more fundamental ; at least it is difficult to imagine
that he will ever attain even the limited and belated
acclamation which has fallen to the lot of the above-
mentioned composers, and, what is more, he seems completely indifferent to the world's praise or censure. Certainly he has never complained or even expressed regret
that with one exception all his large-scale works remain
unpublished and most of them unperformed. Yet I grow
increasingly convinced that Koechlin is among the very
select number of contemporary composers who really
matter—matters, that is, for the intrinsic distinction of
his mind and sensibility, for he has no revolutionary part
to play in musical history. His work has none of the
notoriety value of a Stravinsky or a Schönberg : the apathy
of the musical public—his lack of an audience apart from
a few friends and colleagues—springs not from shock, hostility, or even disapproval, but merely from the failure to

recognize distinction which is remote from any attempt at self-advertisement. Not only has Koechlin made no effort to win popular or critical approval, but, furthermore, there is no trace in his music of the 'bitterness' which is supposed to afflict the contemporary artist, more particularly when he has no, or is suspicious of his, audience. Although remote, Koechlin's music is of a self-subsistent serenity that is singular in contemporary art, almost the only intimation of 'modernity' consisting in a feeling that his fastidiousness is at times so extreme as to become, in the modern world, unreal and almost precious ; and this, I think, is a feeling which dissipates on closer acquaintance with the nature and extent of his *œuvre*.

No composer, not even Fauré, Roussel or Satie, is more intensely and completely French than Koechlin ; like the two former, although, as we shall see, in a rather more specialized sense[1], he is an apostle of French civilization. This remark is not merely a vague reference to the feeling of his music ; it has definite technical implications. Perhaps no other composer's idiom has more direct affiliations both with French folk song and with the evolving tradition of French art music, and yet Koechlin has not so much adapted the elements of the past as taken his place, in an entirely personal way, in that great succession, for no composer has an idiom more immediately and strikingly original. A convenient starting-point for the examination of this idiom is the series of easy pieces for the piano, the sonatinas (dedicated to his children), and the *sonatines*

1 Koechlin studied under Fauré and was his disciple in his fastidiousness and Frenchness and in his disdain for the crowd; but although Fauré's late works were never popularly accepted or understood their idiom was sufficiently reconcilable with the nineteenth-century idiom of the early compositions for them to be accorded a kind of bemused homage. Fauré was respected as a figure of professional dignity, a hub of French musical life; whereas Koechlin, whose idiom, except in the general direction of being French and fastidious, bears no relation to that of Fauré or to that of any contemporary composer, was ostracized as much by the academic as by the fashionable.

françaises for piano duet—none of them work on which his significance rests, but all beautiful and charming, containing some of the fundamentals of his art.

The first and most important feature of these works is that they are music of childhood in so far as they express, like some of Satie's work, an essential innocence, a virginal naïveté of spirit, though without any of Satie's adult, sophisticated, ironic contortion of tonality. The themes themselves are intimately related to the French nursery song and are, save for an occasional 'vocal' modalism of flattened seventh or flattened or (in minor tonalities) sharpened sixth, limpidly diatonic throughout. The lilting rhythms, particularly the six-eight of the children's *ronde*, are of an airy dancing movement that remains, though delicately balanced, exquisitely fluid; the movements are written without regular barring, although the rhythms are never elaborate or congested. The extreme limpidity of the themes is achieved through their symmetry, through the prevalance of conjunct motion mingled with the intervals of fourth and fifth, and through their complete lack of chromaticism—all typical features of French folksong itself; and this luminous consonance is carried over into the harmonic texture which depends largely on the appropriate placing of the bare fourth, fifth, or (with occasional subtlety) second, and on the deceptive minor cadence of French folk-song. The modulations have an instinctive leaning towards the dominant and sub-dominant props of diatonicism, but they may, since the modal progressions have little respect for the orthodox harmonic copybook, become recondite without losing their tender clarity, in so far as they are defined by a fluid contrapuntal movement (*cf.* the first movement of Sonatine 3). None of the movements shows any tendency to sonata 'architecture': either they are very brief binary dance pieces or else they are contrapuntal and in particular canonic—free extensions of the nursery 'catch'. In the duet works the only extended movements are fugal or polyphonic, though on dancing folky rhythms exquisitely cultivated and urbane in effect, the antithesis of the pinchbeck Shropshire Laddery of the rural cult in this country.

I am inclined to think that French folk-song has always been as much more easily assimilated by the 'serious' artist as it is less self-subsistent, less richly varied, than English. However this may be, the airiness of the texture in these works invites comparison with the French chansons of the fifteenth and sixteenth centuries, another sophisticated art which is yet innocent, intimately related to French folk-song, and essentially founded on the consonance of the diatonic triad. Indeed, it might be said that Koechlin has transmuted the spirit of the vocal school of Jannequin or of Claudin de Sermisy or Guillaume de Costeley— perhaps the most fastidiously aristocratic composers in an age of French musical aristocracy—into terms of the keyboard; for the piano writing, usually in two or three parts, has a lovely translucence which in sonorous effect is closer to French sixteenth century vocal writing than to anything usually intimated by the phrase 'keyboard technique'. Hardly is it an influence at all; rather a mode of feeling reborn, and in a different medium. The following quotations will illustrate all these qualities—the radiant diatonicism, the delicate consonance of the harmony, the reticent poetry of the poised yet flowing rhythms, the effect of sunlit distance:

Very occasionally there is a simultaneous merging of unrelated diatonic triads which presages an aspect of the technique of the larger works :

but although they have a subtlety that yields its secret only after intensive acquaintance these are works so immediately attractive and charming that nothing, surely, can prejudice their popular acceptance except the fact that pianists never play them, presumably because they offer no spectacular appeal. The child-like integrity of the vision is important because I think it is only through some such quality that music so serenely innocent could have been written in the twentieth century. If you like, it is an intentional exclusiveness : but it is not an 'escape'.

These little pieces are more important for what they tell us about Koechlin than intrinsically. Certainly we could not proceed to the study of Koechlin's representative work without having referred to them as a statement of certain fundamentals. Another published piano work, the *Paysages et Marines,* provides an approach to the mature idiom, so we must examine this music in some detail.

If there is no excuse for the neglect of the sonatinas, one must admit that the *Paysages et Marines* are undeniably difficult and inaccessible. Familiarity has gradually convinced me that they are among the few outstanding piano works of our time. As an introduction one might point out that Koechlin is a musicologist of considerable learning, and that mediaeval music, particularly that of France, is among his chief enthusiasms. To the diatonic French tonal feeling already noticed is now added a plasticity and freedom of line and a fluid polymodality which has some relation to mediaeval music (the most extreme example is *Le Chevrier*); and this is accompanied by an extension of harmonic resource which, however polyharmonic, none the less preserves its root in the absolute consonances. Throughout this music the atmospheric effect still owes much of its luminosity and serenity to flowing, calm figures founded on conjunct motion and on the intervals of fourth and fifth and the almost complete avoidance of chromaticism : but now the lines have often no clearly defined tonal centre, or they may have several such centres at once, as they become much longer and more plastic. The counterpoint becomes curiously hollow, even heterophonic, on a basis of fourths and fifths, and sometimes the lines are doubled in fourths or fifths or tripled in major or minor triads, as in organum, only in more than one part simultaneously, producing extremely dissonant clashes between chords that are in themselves almost always fundamental consonances. Two superimposed fifths or fourths (creating natural ninths or sevenths) often move in parallel motion to enhance the effect of melting radiance not by their dissonance but by a more expansive conception of consonance. This civilized,

Machaut-like 'mediaeval' element is, of course, not
archaistic: but it gives to this French-founded music a
European cultivation which can be found also in some
of the work of Roussel, but which is lacking in the very
beautiful but relatively more restricted, local and topical
modality and organum of Vaughan Williams' Pastoral
Symphony. A somewhat lengthy quotation from *Soir
d'Eté* will illustrate how the 'vocal' nature of the themes,
their modal and rhythmic plasticity, the fluid dissonance
of the mingling organum effects and consonant harmonies,
and the hollowness of the polyphony, give to the music
a peculiarly transfigured, rarefied atmosphere:

The serenity of the children's pieces is still there, but it
has lost its warmth and smiling quietude; its pastoral

lyricism has become more tenuous as it has become a more
completely adult, and therefore difficult, experience. But
it is remarkable that even where the polyharmonic combinations of chords become most abstruse, as in this
quotation from *Paysage d'Octobre* :

the effect of consonance is never entirely relinquished
because, so consummate is the placing of the chords on
the keyboard that it remains possible to hear the components on, as it were, more than one plane simultaneously.
Even the rare and exceptional appearance of the
sensuous diminished seventh chord earlier in this piece,
and the occasional use of the static, 'Debussyan' ninth
in (for instance) *Poème Virgilien* or in the ravishing closing
section of *Chanson des Pommiers*, acquire, within the
characteristic texture, an unusually impersonal clarity.
Indeed, the harmony, like the polyphony, always remains
closer in spirit to the linear idiom of the fourteenth and
fifteenth centuries than to the advanced chromaticisms
of the nineteenth, 'poetical' though the atmosphere may be ;
the *Chant de Pêcheur*, one of the typical triplet *ronde
française* melodies, contains some astonishingly uncompromising passages in parallel fourths and, finally, seconds.
I know of no music more unearthly in atmosphere ; that
more implies, 'atmospheric' though it is, the relinquish-
ment of the senses. With one ambiguous exception all the
pieces are in slow tempo and fortes are rare ; to listen to
the pieces in sequence (which is how they should be
played) is so oddly disturbing, if perhaps enervating, an
experience that no question of monotony of mood is
involved.

Two other published piano works—the 24 *Esquisses* and the 12 *Pastorales*—reconcile two manners—the gentle warmth and nursery-tune melodic naïveté of the sonatinas with something of the mediaeval-seeming spirituality, the fluid modality, the extremely plastic rhythms and the superimposed harmonies of the *Paysages et Marines*. Some of the pieces are lucidly diatonic, but with rather more sophisticated (even delicately chromatic) harmonies than in the sonatines (*cf.* most of the pieces in the first set of *Esquisses*); others are as simply modal as an early French carol (*cf.* No. 5 from the first set of *Esquisses*). Others again are as free in both their tonal transitions and rhythms and as recondite in their groupings of chords as anything in the *Paysages,* though the texture generally remains lighter (*cf.* most of the *Pastorales* and all the slow pieces in the second book of *Esquisses*). Although less remarkable than the *Paysages et Marines,* these are compositions of great beauty and distinction, and are perhaps in a sense more representative in that the reconciliation of tendencies that Koechlin here effects in a slight fashion is to be found in a much more significant form in his large-scale compositions—those on which his importance rests. It is the application of this technique to the big works that we have now to consider.

Of these compositions, only one—the violin and piano sonata—is published, but that is an entirely representative instance, sufficient to establish both the mastery and originality of Koechlin's idiom. None of the movements is in 'dramatic' sonata form, the whole work being relatively melodic and polyphonic. It begins with a short, slow movement, 'calme, lumineux, et féerique'. The opening will indicate the characteristic beauty of the themes, long, flowing, non-chromatic, built on conjunct motion combined with fourths and fifths; the glowing radiance of the harmonic structure, with its clear major triads and superimposed perfect consonances :

The movement develops in an entirely linear fashion, the texture becoming increasingly polymodal, with organum effects in the middle parts. But despite the poly-harmonies and the extremely fluid tonal extensions of the line—of which the following is representative :

—the atmosphere of paradisal calm is preserved throughout. This movement is remarkable not only for the beauty of its linear substance, but as a unique experiment in tonal balance—though perhaps the two aspects are hardly separable. It is certain that never before has the apparently crude combination of violin and modern concert grand attained quite this ethereal unworldly appositeness. It is extremely difficult to play.

This originality of sonorous quality dominates the second movement also—a long scherzo. The themes—of the triplet *ronde* type—are hinted at only very tentatively in the midst of some pentatonic arabesques and muted trills on the violin and fluttering pianissimo arpeggios in fourths on the piano, sometimes accompanied by bare fifths harmonically unrelated. The texture of the writing for both instruments is tremulous and shimmering,

and the main theme, when eventually it emerges, is
unexpectedly warm, supple and caressing (see violin part
of quotation below). Extensive developments of this theme
are melodic and polyphonic rather than thematic, pliant
lyrical phrases continually generating variations of rhythm
and modality. The increased richness of the tonal transitions and harmonic texture at the climaxes—still founded
largely on superimposed fourths and fifths—is indicated
in the following quotation :

The lyricism finally quivers away in some whispered trills
for the violin and scurrying arpeggio triads for the piano,
followed by a reference to the opening in crystalline unison
writing and two bare fifths in the topmost registers of the
keyboard.

The slow movement is entirely in the manner of the
Paysages et Marines, with the addition, of course, of an
extended lyrical part—a restrained soaring meditation—
for the violin. The final section may be quoted because of
its exquisite organum effect in superimposed fifths, the
loveliness of the line, and the clarity of the placing of the
diatonic triads :

With the finale we come to the longest and most important movement, an elaborately polyphonic rondo. The main theme, reminiscent of a French dance tune, is stated immediately accompanied by bare fifths; the first episode is a free polyphonic passage that has affinities with the polyphony of the fourteenth and fifteenth centuries:

Conjunct motion and a suave vocal disposition of the intervals prevail, but the tonalities grow increasingly ambiguous as all the material is extended and developed with much canonic complication and at considerable length. The following may be quoted as an example of the texture at the climaxes—again a completely original treatment of the piano-violin combination, though one very difficult to perform convincingly :

Some hint of the technique of lyrical generation in the violin line is given here; and in general the method of development is a polymodal and polyharmonic extension of free fifteenth century polyphony, into which references to the original symmetrical dance tune are interjected.

After a series of canonic stretti in elliptical tonalities there is a long tumultuous coda over whirling arpeggio fifths, the tonality of B major is reinstated (the movement had opened in D, the relative major of B minor), and the work finds its peroration in a *large* statement of the main melody over resonant diatonic triads, sometimes with added seconds. It is remarkable that although the sonorous power of parts of the movement, especially the close, is immense, the impression of luminosity and clarity remains because, for all the modal ambiguities and polyharmonies, the absolute and perfect consonances are still the roots of the tonal structure. The music gives a sensation of intensely white light, and the writing for the instruments is unique and entirely beautiful, provided that the performers are of sufficiently rarefied spiritual, as well as technical, accomplishment.

None of Koechlin's other major works is published, so I cannot discuss them in any detail. The chamber works include sonatas for cello, viola, oboe, clarinet, flute, bassoon and horn, all with piano. The flute sonata, though naturally slighter than the violin work, manifests the same mastery of sonorous quality, the same personal luminosity; the horn work is one of the loveliest incarnations of this beautiful instrument—so congenial to Koechlin's characteristic sonority—in existence, and ought to be published if only because the repertoire for the horn is so scanty. The other sonatas I have never heard.

Koechlin has also composed a quintet for piano and strings, a sonata for two unaccompanied flutes, and three string quartets in his suave brand of mediaeval-seeming polyphony. There are a number of unpublished piano works, including a *Ballade,* and a considerable number of songs. For orchestra his works include *Les Saisons, La Forêt, Etudes Antiques, Chant Funèbre à la memoire des jeunes femmes défunctes,* two ballets, *La Forêt Paienne* and *La Divine Vesper,* and a long and elaborate suite called *Les Heures Persanes;* none of these have I seen or heard. But his masterpiece would seem to be an enormous semi-mystical creation, *L'Abbaye,* for chorus, orchestra and organ, of which the second and more important part is still, I believe, unperformed. The long fluid 'vocal' lines and polyphony, the lucid polyharmonies, the superimposed fourths and fifths which gave to the *Paysages* and the violin sonata their rarefied spirituality are here explored with still greater depth and nobility and the cold, yet sweetly glowing quality of Koechlin's orchestration is without precedent in musical history. With only a scanty knowledge of the first part of the work, I would be prepared to maintain that, although isolated and remote from the main growth of European music, *L'Abbaye* is one of the few masterpieces of the twentieth century, but I am afraid it is one that is never likely to be widely performed.

This, perhaps, prompts the query whether the rarity and

distinction of Koechlin's mind does not imply a deficiency
in what we ordinarily call 'humanity'. It is true that his
spiritually and serenity have not the centrality of Palestrina's or the vigour of Bach's—that *relatively* they seem
'personal' and even precious—but those are hardly comparisons that any contemporary artist could stand up to.
Certainly he seems limited compared with the best of
Fauré or Bartók : but not so limited as the complete
unwillingness of the 'majority' to listen to him might lead
one to believe. His work has been misunderstood mainly
because it is so incompletely known. The piano *sonatines,*
though representative of *some* of the fundamentals of his
art, give no notion of the profoundly transfigured complexity of the *Paysages et Marines;* and these in turn do
not adequately indicate the range and force that may be
embraced within similar 'visionary' experiences in the
large-scale works such as the violin sonata, not to mention
the orchestral works and *L'Abbaye*[2]. If the violin sonata
really is too fastidiously cultivated to be comprehensible
to musical people to-day one can only say, so much the

2 This should not be taken as a chronological distinction nor
as an indication that either the sonatinas or the *Paysages* are in
any way 'immature'. Koechlin allows his imagination to function
on, as it were, several different levels, but in each case the clarity
of the realization is masterly. With the exception of a few very
early and uncharacteristic songs, all the music of Koechlin
which is known to me is of consummate maturity, though it must
be admitted that I am really familiar with his work only after op.
59. The chronology of his music is anyway extremely obscure.
The first part of *L'Abbaye* is numbered op. 16 and the piano
Esquisses op. 41. The piano sonatinas, the *Paysages et Marines,*
the various sonatas, the quartets and quintet extend intermittently
from op. 55 to 82. None of the recognized encyclopædias sheds
any light on the numerous missing quantities; it hardly
seems probable that they are all compositions which Koechlin dis-
owns or has destroyed. The complete ignorance of Koechlin's later
songs, written after he had evolved his personal manner, is particularly regrettable, since one would expect his mastery of this
medium to be uniquely beautiful, and the economic objections
that might be urged against performance of *L'Abbaye* or *Les
Heures Persanes* certainly would not apply in this case.

worse for the people : it is hardly Koechlin's fault. Whatever his final position may be—and we cannot hope to
assess it while most of his big works remain unpublished
and unperformed—he is certainly among the select
number of contemporary composers who have added an
original language to musical history; and, as part of that
language, apposite only to his peculiar purposes, he has
created a personal *timbre*—a mastery of the stuff of sound
—which has a nostalgic purity that is without precedent.
It is because his music preserves, however elaborately polyphonic and polyharmonic it may grow, something of vocal
limpidity both in its French lines and harmonies that it
has an emotional tenor so entirely consistent and of such
virginal charm. However profound, it is never self-con-
sciously soulful; however light and airy, it is never (like
so much twentieth-century French music) knowingly
witty. It *is* a mode of apprehending, both spiritual and
spirituel; this is why, for those willing to listen, its
innocence may provide at times a source of refreshment
which other contemporary composers, even the greater
ones, cannot offer. If the serenity of its innocence implies,
unlike the dismay of the innocence of Satie, a withdrawal
from the world of the present day, at least one cannot
claim that it is the world that has the right to pity.

Music Review 1942.

VI

MAHLER AS KEY-FIGURE

OF THE GREAT COMPOSERS in the history of European music Mahler is, with the solitary exception of Berlioz, the one who has excited the most controversy. Perhaps 'controversy' is a strong word with reference to the tepid defence his few English supporters have been able, until at least the last few years, to put up : yet even in England there has been a notable lack of agreement as to the reasons why Mahler's music is bad, and none of the accepted accounts squares, of course, with the eulogistic, even reverent, attitude to his work which is held, or used to be held, in Austria, Belgium, and Holland.

For instance, we are told that Mahler is an 'old wind-bag' who talked so much about his own tragic feelings that he did not even know what his feelings were ; or, more politely, that though Mahler the tragic sufferer was genuine enough in his emotional outpourings he was essentially the romantic egoist and we (being so much more mature and sophisticated) are not interested in that sort of thing any longer. Conflicting oddly with this individualistic account we have the theory that Mahler is the bourgeois composer *par excellence*, whose aim and function is to 'move masses' ; and Dr. Wellesz's thesis, reflecting the prevalent Austrian opinion, that Mahler is not so much a romantic as the end of the classical tradition.

Now it seems to me that there is an element of truth in all these accounts, and Mahler's significance consists most in that he reconciles them all. His contribution to European musical thought lies in his embracing so much, in his revealing the latent relationships within apparent anomalies—their cross-references in a period of transition.

Let us begin with the most obvious, the sense in which Mahler is indubitably the typical romantic figure. There can be no question that Mahler, as a Jew, was conscious of a sense of isolation; that he did talk somewhat pompously about the state of his soul, that he was aware of all manner of inner conflicts which in his music he attempted to resolve. Nor can there be any question that twentieth-century minds are repelled by the extra-musical philosophizings. Yet it seems to me clear that, after Beethoven, a German composer could only in very exceptional circumstances have avoided a self-dramatizing attitude; and there is a sense in which it is perfectly true to say that 'all music is programme music'. Did Mahler, after all, claim much more than this sense? In a letter to Bruno Walter he once remarked that when he listened to music all his doubts and difficulties vanished and he felt 'entirely clear and sure'—a very revealing sentiment because it suggests that Mahler was aware that his emotional turmoils could have no significance apart from his music. No amount of discussion of the verbal aura can obviate this fact, that the music stands or falls because it is music and until one has listened to and studied it *qua* music—as most of the people in England who used to be so patronizing about it had neither inclination nor opportunity to do—discussion is not only useless but misleading.

If we concentrate, then, on that aspect of Mahler's romanticism which we can locate in musical terms we see that technically it is associated, as the cult of the personal usually is, with the chromatic ('Wagnerian') nature of his harmony, and with the exotic (or colouristic) aspects of his orchestral technique. In this respect Mahler, like Wagner and like Delius, marks the end of a cultural epoch, and we can see how the sunset of his voluptuous harmony and rich orchestration wavers into the twilight of the extreme chromaticism and orchestral exoticisms of early Berg, Schönberg and Webern. The monstrous Beardes-

leyesque orchestration of the *Gurrelieder* and the Berg
Three Orchestral Pieces is a more fantastic extension of the
gorgeous Mahlerian tapestry, while the pointilliste scoring
of Webern's Seven Orchestral Pieces, where the shifting
tone-colour of each note takes on melodic significance,
shows Mahler's exoticism in *reductio ad absurdum*—a
musical expression of the M. Teste element in twentieth-
century art, realized with an attenuated, ghostly validity.

And yet even in Mahler's most romantic work—consider
the beautiful and moving *Kindertotenlieder*—one is aware
of a nervous vitality that over-reaches the representative
egoistical wallow. Technically I think the source of this
strength is in the rhapsodic nature of Mahler's
lyricism, so that one cannot say that even in his most
nineteenth-centuryish compositions—and remember we are
so far examining only Mahler's purely romantic characteristics—Mahler is a poor melodist but rather that in
such passages he is a melodist of a very special type. It
is instructive in this connection to recall the case of Delius,
a composer with whom the romantic Mahler has a good
deal in common. It has always seemed to me that although
it is on the whole the gorgeously shifting chromatic harmony that provides the *modus vivendi* of Delius' music,
the melody yet provides a decorative arabesque which
preserves an authentic lyrical volition; is rhapsodically free if not entirely—because it partly depends for
its effect upon contrast with the rich harmonic background
—a self-subsistent entity. Delius' music is at its best, I
think, when this dual value—the sense at once of independence of and interdependence between melody and
harmony—is most clearly present; and this is why his
finest compositions are those which include a part for
voice or solo instrument. The beautiful Violin Concerto,
in which the soloist's soaring lyricism counter-balances the
orchestra's sonorous harmonic framework, exhibits his
method at its ripest perfection; so, more equivocally, do
Sea-Drift and the powerful Second Violin Sonata. The

melody here does not generate the harmony, as the most
vital kind of melody probably does ; but it is certainly not
correct to say, following the conventional account which
even Mr. Lambert subscribes to, that the harmony generates
the melody. The two are separate yet mutually interdependent and the poised gravity of these works—so much
more mature than the dangerous Delian nostalgia—seems
to me to be due to this equilibrium.

A similar duality is behind the technique of the
romantic Mahler, and here is the real significance of his
repeated introduction of the solo voice into his symphonic
work. Mahler's solo parts in his symphonies explore the
possibilities of vocal declamation in lyrical arabesque with
the utmost subtlety of nuance—consider the exquisite
Autumn movement from *Das Lied von der Erde,* where
the contralto solo inter-twines into the mesh of orchestral
fabric a silvery line of expressively meditative pathos ; a
line which, hovering on the brink of tonality,
adds harmonic piquancies to the texture of the
orchestral score. I believe this rhapsodic lyricism is the
technical equivalent of the quality Mr. Henry Boys referred
to when he spoke, in his notes to the H.M.V. recording
of the Ninth Symphony, of the conventional nature of
Mahler's rhetoric and its relation to the baroque tradition
in Austrian art. Mahler's rhetoric may not after all be so
much the product of vulgar sentimentality (as the purely
harmonic account would indicate) as a convention as
legitimate as that of (say) the rhetoric of Elizabethan
drama. Obviously the achievement is bound to be a delicate
one ; and even one of his finest works, *Das Lied,* seems to
me to fall in parts of the first movement into a relatively
cheap emotionalism that is ever so slightly reminiscent of
Puccini. But when successful, as in the oriental *melismata*
passages from the *Farewell* of *Das Lied,* it is a convention
that justifies itself supremely.

These wonderful *melismata* passages tend away
from diatonicism to a linear rather than harmonic concep-

tion. Often with a pronounced pentatonic feeling, or in
elaborate metrical periods similar to those of asiatic music,
with a characteristic use of internal pedals, they indicate
how Mahler's romantic rhapsody implies a notion of his
art which links its comparatively local and topical harmonic
elements both with the polyphonic past and the linear
future. The romantic account, if offered alone, is revealed
as patently unsatisfactory; and we are now in a position
to examine his relation to musical tradition.

I suppose the most obvious, the simplest relation is
his connection with Austrian folk-song. This is behind
many of the passages that are stigmatized as 'vulgar'
and are supposed to be so outlandish in works designed
to incarnate experience of tragic profundity. But
Mahler approached folk-song in no antiquarian spirit; in
one aspect the individualistic Mahler was still one of the
Folk himself, just as Schubert had been, with the mould
and inflexion of their songs in his blood and bones. As an
honest creator he could not have kept the song-spirit
out of his music even if he had wanted to; because he
was interested first of all in the making of music he knew
that he could not solve his 'difficulties' by denying his
personality. Phantasmal and almost macabre as the great
Ländler movement of the Ninth Symphony becomes in
the course of its evolution, we can see that even up to 1911,
the year in which Mahler died, the kinship with folk-song
is still potent. Traces of a feudal conception of society
survived in Austria, of course, beyond Mahler's death until
the Great War of 1914; since Mahler spent the creative
periods of his life—the summer months—in the country,
he would have had plenty of first-hand experience of
native song and dance.

A second point with reference to Mahler's connection
with the past is his Roman Catholicism. For all his
spiritual turmoils (technically represented by his preoccupation with the nineteenth-century dramatic aspect
of the symphonic ideal) he preserved contact with a

H

Catholic, European, polyphonic musical culture, so that
the great Choral Symphony (No. 8) is in one sense—
though it is as we shall see many other things also—one of
the last *big* works to be composed under the influence
of a stable religious belief. Of course, his Catholicism did
not recommend itself conspicuously to the moral and cultural fashions of the decade after his death; I think it is
true to say that the incomprehension of his music so
arrogantly displayed during this period is due as much to
the traditionally religious aspect of his art as to the
notoriously unpopular element of personality.

This polyphonic aspect of Mahler's work is intimately
associated with the most important of these links with
Europe's musical past—his connection with the classical
symphonic tradition. Although Mahler's music represents
the end of an epoch and is elegiac in feeling, we must
remember that it marks the end of a particular civilization
—an Austrian culture centred in Vienna, so that
he is the last of the great line that, beginning with
Haydn, extended through Mozart, Schubert, Beethoven,
Bruckner; and in this sense Mahler is not so much a
rhapsodist as a lyrical melodist in his own right. What,
however, is most interesting is precisely how Mahler
adapts the classical convention, reconciles it with the
other elements of his complex personality; and I think
it is by examining this point that we arrive at the core of
Mahler's contribution.

He starts with the Haydnesque symmetrical phrase : but
he injects into the classical phrase something of his personal quality of rhapsodic exaltation, with immense leaps
and drooping suspensions; stretches and modifies it until
the terminal form of the melody is revealed only by a
process of gradual accumulation. In so doing the phrase
inevitably loses its polished balanced urbanity, becomes a
structure relatively plastic and asymmetrical, implying in
its length and freedom a tendency away from the diatonic
dominant-tonic relation towards a more polyphonic notion

of technique. One facet of this is exemplified in the composer's increasing preoccupation with orchestration as the significant delineation of each particular part. The Italian element in Mahler—conspicuous in most representative Austrian art—is here explicit, and the wheel has come full circle. For Haydn's warm and glowing periods had clipped the free vocal phrase of the sixteenth and seventeenth century Italian madrigalists into the symmetrical diatonic instrumental phrase. Starting from Hadyn, Mahler stretches out the phrase, loosens it, until he arrives once more at principles having analogies with those which were implicit in the music of the Italian polyphonists. To reconcile these principles with the dramatic symphonic ideal was the real struggle—or at least the musical manifestation of it—behind his working life. After the choral symphony one would have thought that he could not again tackle an instrumental form; that he did so indicates how complex was the problem, how indirect the solution.

The first movement of the Ninth Symphony, perhaps Mahler's most stupendous creation, might be said to symbolize the struggle, for the whole movement, embracing as it does Mahler's most astounding excursions into a linear atonality that carries us into a new, strange and unearthly universe, is enclosed within a gigantic dominant-tonic progression. Here is the exhaustive working out of the problem which Schubert had tentatively touched on in the lyrical nature and breadth of his subjects in the great posthumous piano sonatas—works whose 'heavenly length' is usually ascribed to the 'inspired' composer's incapacity to deal with the academic forms, despite the fact that his sketch-books have now revealed that he took the utmost pains over them and was aware, however partial his success, of what he was trying to do. The notorious length of Mahler's symphonic movements, with their groups of melodic motives rather than themes, is a phenomenon more extreme than, but directly parallel to, the case of Schubert : not at all due to congenital garrulousness but to the nature of the problem with which he was obsessed.

Mahler arrived, then, at a technique recovering contact with that of the Italian madrigalists : but he was not to sing with their proud faith or their clear serenity. For one thing, he was by this time pitifully ill, and he worked in the conditions that immediately preceded the collapse of the old Austrian régime : deeper than this, and more far-reaching, he lived in a more self-conscious age. Though he transcended he did not dispense with his quality of personal rhapsody; and his polyphony, once achieved, drooped, in the music of his last years posterior to the Eighth Symphony, into a mournful fragmentariness that shows how heavy with world-weariness the wings of his lyricism have grown. This fragmentariness is distinct from the harmonic disintegration of chromaticism, for it is linearly, melodically conceived ; it is a polyphony that bursts with its rhapsodic exaltation or with its pathos bitterly breaks. It is not the stable voice of a Palestrina or a Bach : but it has this much in common with them, that whereas harmonic chromaticism, in Wagner or Delius or in some of Mahler's own earlier work, usually represents a personal preoccupation with and disruption of the senses, the piteous melodic fragmentariness of the coda to the Adagio of the Ninth Symphony is more than personal and sensuous and may be said to symbolize the disintegration of a whole world—of a conception of society and a mode of belief.

The end of a world : and yet, it may be also, the birth-pangs of a new. For just as the chromatic-harmonic and orchestral-exotic elements of Mahler's work look forward to those elements in the work of Schönberg, Berg and Webern which are the last nocturnal glimmer of romanticism, so the fragmentary polyphony of his final compositions looks forward to those elements in the music of the atonalists which are expressive of a strange realm of feel-

ing, a newly awakened sense, which may yet play an
important evolutionary part in music's future. Already,
these elements are present in Mahler, glassily, dangerously calm in their other-worldliness, their linear
angularity, their translucency of texture. The precise
degree of this evolutionary significance is difficult to
estimate, since we cannot speculate with conviction upon
the direction which the formulation of musical language
will take. I have written elsewhere of Edmund Rubbra's
attempt to deal with the same symphonic-polyphonic
problem that preoccupied Mahler, perhaps the most deep-
seated of all the problems of contemporary music : and it
may be that his stable and traditional solution—
tending towards the re-creation of the old modal and
diatonic technique rather than (like Mahler's) towards the
search for a new language through the dissipation of the
old—offers the most fruitful as well as, in a sense,
the most logical way out. On the other hand,
the culture of the future, if there is any, may well
be of an order such that Rubbra's traditionalism would be,
for all the freshness of its contemporary re-creation,
inappropriate to it; pretty certainly such culture will be
relatively amorphous and international. In this case the
twelve-note technique, and behind it some aspects of the
work of Mahler, might have more than the iconoclastic
significance of having destroyed, by unequivocally accepting equal temperament and thereby establishing the
absolute liberty of the semitone, the harmonic conceptions
on which European music has been based for some nine
centuries. It might, in the course of time, lead to a new
linear conception of music founded, like the music of Asia
and the Orient, on microtonal inflexions within a framework of the absolute consonances. The rhythmic flaccidity
of some twelve-note music may possibly be a kind of
growing-pain which music is suffering in passing from the
relatively time-obsessed European rhythmic sense to something resembling the almost ungraspably slow rhythmic

periods of (say) Japanese music. Certainly the polyrhythmic experiments of the Americans would be relevant to the evolution of such a music and, for better or worse, it is at least feasible that the music of a vast international society such as we envisage might resemble the timeless and placeless music of eastern civilizations more than the comparatively topical and local idioms of European music as we have so far known it, though it would have, of course, to be an entirely indigenous product.

Perhaps, should musical history take this course, the most significant composer with reference to the *immediate* future of musical language will be Bartók. For the technique explored in his recent works reconciles a legitimate extension of the classical, eighteenth-century, melodic conception of dissonance with principles of line-drawing comparable with those of Asiatic music, so that he provides, as it were, a compromise, a half-way house, between two musical worlds—not so much between western and eastern as between the traditional European world and the hypothetical, more international, future that may be presaged in some duodecuple music.

However this may be—and it is too early, yet, to tell— the salvation of the symphony symbolized in Rubbra's No. 3, or the disintegration of it symbolized in Mahler's No. 9, offer a choice of ways of more than technical significance. We can see, in this remarkable Ninth Symphony of Mahler, the main problems of European music—the polyphonic principle of the sixteenth century, the symphonic ideal of the classical tradition, the nineteenth-century cult of the personal and dramatic, the baroque notion of rhetoric, the twentieth-century explorations into an 'unterrestrial' linear counterpoint—all touched upon and synthesized. I doubt if there is any single work that can shed more light upon the difficulties of the composer in relation to the contemporary world. And it contains music wild and passionate and painfully beautiful which only those whose response has been atrophied by our sophisticated refusal to feel anything without the 'ironic' protection of intellectual canniness, can fail to recognize as the expression of a spirit at once noble and incisive; of an age which, if in some respects outmoded, has much to teach us if ever the 'new world' so frequently discussed is to be, in reality, born.

Scrutiny 1940.

VII

EGON WELLESZ AND THE
AUSTRIAN TRADITION

THE GENERAL EXODUS OF talent and distinction
which Hitler's New Order in Germany inaugurated might
be expected to yield some interesting results; interesting,
that is, to the countries which provide a temporary refuge
or permanent haven to the banished men of genius. It is,
then, the more disturbing that the most important creative
musician to come to this country from Austria has had to
remain for more than six years completely neglected. I do
not know why this should be so, unless it is that the nineteenth-century notion that it is dangerous for a musician
to have brains is here peculiarly deeply rooted; for Egon
Wellesz happens to be not only one of the most distinguished members of the Schönberg group, but also a
musicologist of considerable learning; and in the latter
field we have not been slow to honour him.

So I had better point out what should by now be a
truism, that there is nothing odd about a composer thinking about his craft. Indeed to-day it would be odd if, to
some degree at least, the composer *didn't* think; for the
contemporary artist is unavoidably more or less self-
conscious. Without a mutual reciprocity between composer
and society—whereby all music is in the main contemporary music—the composer is bound to think about his
postulates. Palestrina, Bach or Mozart all worked hard to
acquire the technical skill within which their originality
manifested itself, but they none of them had any doubts
about the kind of skill they wanted; their idiom, their
criterion, was presented to them by society, and an
inestimably valuable gift it was. The contemporary com-

poser has to arrive at his own idiom; and he cannot but
realize that his own problems cannot be separated
from wider problems covering not only all aspects of
musical education, but the whole cultural background
against which these problems exist. To-day, the composer
cannot afford to be exclusively a specialist.

Granting that there is nothing strange, especially nowadays, about a composer thinking, not merely the fact of
their existence, but the nature of Wellesz's researches
becomes extremely interesting. His musicological work has
been centred in Byzantine music and in seventeenth-
century baroque opera; and both these have a significant
bearing on European cultural history. Relatively without
bearings of his own, the contemporary composer looks back
to consider his relations to the past. If he is to be conscious
of the past it must be the past viewed in a sane perspective,
not merely the last two centuries of it : moreover, since his
path is likely to be one of exploration rather than of acceptance, he will be interested in conceptions of music quite
alien to those on which he has been nurtured. Wellesz sees
Europe's past as that of a predominantly Christian
community; he looks at the music of the Middle Ages,
the supreme periods of Christian faith; beyond that he
looks at the merging of our Christian traditions of the west
with those of the east. He sees in Byzantine music the point
where two worlds meet—the music of the Christian tradition against its timeless non-Christian background.

In the connection between music and the Church—
between music and belief—is the most fundamental of
all relations between music and society; in the music and
ritual of the mass the human drama assumes cosmological
form. But when the Catholic world-view weakens as a
social force and the stress shifts gradually from the universe
of God which contains all individual souls, to the
humanistic view of the central significance of the individual
soul itself, the chief social manifestation of music moves
from the Church to the stage. Perhaps it is not

fanciful to suggest that the change from the polyphonic outlook in which music is a concourse of equally
important voices to the homophonic approach in which
one voice is the leader (with the growing importance of
harmony as a medium for dramatic expressiveness) is not
unconnected with this modification of world-view.
Certainly the brilliant baroque decoration and the development of expressive harmonically underlined recitative
which we find in seventeenth-century opera make this
music one of the most crucial manifestations of the musical
beginnings of the modern world. Wellesz's dominant
musicological interests thus centre around the most fundamental problems with which the contemporary composer
has to deal : on the one hand his relation to belief and
the Christian past, and the connection of that with music
and civilizations other than our own ; on the other hand
the critical years at the beginning of the seventeenth century when the mediaeval world was well-nigh disintegrated,
but when the individualism of the new world was still
vitally in contact with tradition. Perhaps we may say the
opera—the conscious discovery of the relation between
music and language, and therefore life—became necessary only when the more intuitive union of man's various
fields of creativity, characteristic of the early religious
society, had all but passed away.

This may seem a circuitous approach to Wellesz's
creative work, but I wished to demonstrate how inseparably
his musicological interests are bound up with his own
problems as a composer ; and how these in turn are to
varying degrees every composer's problems. When Wellesz
started on his career he was working in the atmosphere
which had produced the cultural phenomenon of
Parsifal and the deliquescence of diatonic tonality. But
Vienna had a saving strength which the Wagnerians as a
whole lacked, in that it was in contact with an instrumental
tradition which did not blindly accept Wagner's premises.
The line ran from the Italian baroque opera composers

to the Viennese symphonists—to Haydn, Mozart, Beethoven, Bruckner and Schubert. It is this tradition which was shortly to sing its swan song in the Ninth Symphony of Mahler; it is this tradition which implicitly helped to give such vitality to the early *fin-de-siècle* work of Schönberg and Berg, such as the *Gurrelieder* and the Three Orchestral Pieces, with their enormous orchestras and sumptuous exotic colouring; and the first works of Wellesz show a similar merging of idioms. Very early came the realization that in the passive acceptance of a creed emphasizing the all importance of nervous sensation and of personal emotion lay the danger of a kind of corrupt emotional inflation of which *Parsifal* was by no means an isolated, or the worst, example. This led not at first to any direct modification of the æsthetic but to a tendency away from the Wagnerian opulence and towards greater sensitivity and delicacy in the conveyance of nervous sensation. In the case of Schönberg the tendency took the form of the pointillism of the first completely atonal works—away from the magnificent but over-ripe Wagnerianism of the string sextet or the magnificent but over-ripe Brahmsianism of the first quartet to a type of linear atonality divested of harmonic implications—even chromatic ones. The effect—consummated in *Pierrot Lunaire*—was still essentially nervous; but the texture was now taut, glittering, precise. Wellesz did not follow this path. With him the search for delicacy and precision brought with it the influence of Debussy's impressionism, with a discreet use of the higher chromatic discords and a prevalence of organum-like effects and pentatonic figuration. The mingling of oriental elements with the parnassianism of Stefan George assumes an increased significance when we reflect on Wellesz's subsequent development; and the works of this period do indeed contain much music of exquisite beauty in which the characteristic Wellesz sonority is clearly established— great fluidity and sensitivity to speech inflection in the melodic line, a curious tingling, glinting quality in the chromatic arabesques and decorations.

But this phase—for Schönberg, Berg and Wellesz—could be only transitional. All felt the need to organize their music on a bigger and more disciplined scale than the mere transference into sound, however beautiful, of the quiverings of the nervous system. All chose the theatre as the obvious medium wherein a musical sensuousness might be developed in terms of human significance; but a human and dramatic discipline must imply a musical discipline too, and gradually Schönberg evolved the *musical* formalism of the twelve-note technique. Wellesz chose a different method—the reconciliation of the pointillist technique not perhaps with the immediate diatonic past which Wagner and the early atonal work had splintered, but with the more distant European past out of which that diatonicism had grown. Schönberg and Berg countered the Wagnerian convention of emotional elephantiasis by insisting on the most rigorous eighteenth-century musical formalism within the theatrical convention; Wellesz aimed to recreate the theatrical convention itself. He sought a return to the merging of music in stylized spectacle, drama, poetry and dance such as had characterized early baroque opera and ballet; and like Gluck, he wished to combine the maximum amount of psychological and ethical penetration with the most effective musical stylization. This reborn operatic classicism in some ways parallels Mahler's re-creation of the Viennese symphonic tradition through the interplay of Italian baroque rhetoric.

The works of this period are thus an advance beyond personal sensation in their classical lay-out, with ritualized gestures, ballet technique and stylized choruses; in their ethical significance; and in the nature of the musical idiom itself. The characteristic chromatic splintering of tonality to achieve a close approximation to speech inflection is always balanced by a desire to *objectify* nervous tensions which produces an insistence on ferocious motor-rhythms (connecting up, theatrically, with the dance element) remote from the flaccidity typical of early atonalism. And while the nervous chromatic figurations remain, they have become arabesque-like convolutions around a texture which achieves a high degree of dissonance through the uncompromising polytonal organization of diatonic lines. The 'classical' basis is felt as latent; and it is through the convention of baroque ornament that the sensuous 'atonal' figurations are reconciled with a monumental sense of classical harmonic design, and with the powerful instinct for physical movement. Wellesz has solved the problem of creating an urgently, even aggressively, contemporary music in a framework which implies at once a social and ethical conscience and a respect for the traditions of the past. If the anguished rhythmic ferocity of parts of the music seem to overweigh the more positive acceptance of some of the tranquil solo passages with their 'religious' pentatonic and modal feeling, its uncompromising honesty and power are the condition of the composer's development. The acceptance is to come.

In Vienna, where there was a still flourishing operatic tradition, it was natural that Wellesz should devote his main attention to re-creating the social and ethical implications of his art in musico-dramatic form. For the modern world the connection between music and the stage is, or should be, as we have seen, the most important link of music with life. But both the ethical nature of Wellesz's operatic ventures, and at times, especially in solo and choral passages, the nature of the music itself, remind us that Wellesz has never forgotten the still deeper (however difficult for a contemporary artist) relation between music and life, namely, its function in the church. Significantly after he had completed the big Greek trilogy Wellesz deserted opera for a time and produced a series of church works actually intended for liturgical use. For Wellesz sees his church music as a social and religious *activity*, not as a form to write in : and because the works are for liturgical use the idiom must necessarily be relatively simple. The atonal figurations either disappear or become, as in late Mahler, anguished unresolved appoggiaturas with tonal implications; the idiom is rooted in the vocal modes and instrumental diatonicism. The choral writing derives, by way of the Lutheran Bach, from a continuous Austrian Catholic tradition harking back, through Isaac, to late mediaeval polyphony, with occasional polytonal modifications in the part writing. The solo arias and instrumental passages are a free polytonal extension from the baroque lyricism of Bach and Buxtehude; with perfect appropriateness the gigantic leaps of Mahler's or Schönberg's line are assimilated into this idiom to obtain effects of cumulative climax. The energetic motor-rhythms calm down; the structure is clearly defined on the models of mediaeval motet, the baroque concerto grosso and cantata. For all its intimate relation to the past and the subjects of Wellesz's researches, the music is of impressive originality, whether in the big cantata and masses, or in the tiny but at the same time massively powerful choral pieces from Silesius. But again this is a transitional phase; the exploration of the religious relation between music and the community and the discipline of liturgical use (even the big cantata is intended for festival performance) were essential if Wellesz was fully to realize the implications of his ethical approach to music drama. Ironically enough this masterly realization has come, after a silence of several years, when the country in which he was born, nurtured and honoured has turned its back on him; and mostly in a country in which opera is not an accepted part of the life of the community. That these works are not actually in dramatic form does not alter the fact that they are an assured solution of the problems posed in the operatic works. The intensity and exploration of the operas and ballets are here married to the lucidity of the church works. Clarity of realization is achieved without any sacrifice (to some extent inevitable in the liturgical pieces) of complexity and profundity.

An anticipation of Wellesz's most recent development is to be found in the Elizabeth Barrett Browning Sonnets for voice and string quartet (1934). Here is probably Wellesz's supreme accomplishment in vocal line; and like Monteverdi, he chromatically disintegrates a stable vocal line into speech inflection only so that the tensity of the expression may weld the fragments into a lyricism the more moving in that it arises out of the most subtle appreciation of verbal stress. Of course unlike Monteverdi, and like Bach, the vocal writing is greatly influenced by instrumental technique, while the very polyphonic string parts gain in pliancy through their relation to the speech inflection of the vocal line; this reciprocity, so important in the German tradition since Bach, surely here reaches one of its most maturely sensitive forms. The calm concluding bars also illustrate the cathartic effect of the latent diatonicism beneath the baroque atonal figuration.

But it is with a large-scale orchestral work *Prosperos Beschworungen (Prospero's Spells)* (1936-38), that the 'late' manner is fully inaugurated. Significantly, though a purely orchestral composition, this work is in essence dramatic and ethical; perhaps it took this form because opera had become impracticable[1]. It is scored for a big orchestra with a truly virtuoso clarity, and includes almost every facet of Wellesz's art—the extraordinarily sensitive atonal-baroque lyrical writing (we may quote the opening of Ariel's Song) :

1   Since writing the above Dr. Wellesz has informed me that he conceived the idea of an opera on Shakespeare's *Tempest* in 1927, but abandoned it largely owing to the impracticable number of subsidiary characters. *Prospero's Spells* was thus the result of ten years' imaginative 'brewing' of the *Tempest* themes.

the cumulative rhythmic excitement (Caliban); the
wavering pentatonic-tending heterophonic writing which
reminds one at once of mediaeval lyricism and of the late
work of Mahler, combining as it does the local elements
in Wellesz's art with the European (we may refer to the
exquisite, melting, Prospero and Miranda section with its
explicit D flat major basis); and the careful formal
organization within which the psychological subtlety manifests itself. That Ariel's theme is a modification of Prospero's
because he is an emanation of his master is a kind of organization which is both inherently musical and philosophical.
The concentrated epilogue also shows the same fusion of
musical with imaginative and dramatic insight.

Prospero is one of Wellesz's most complex works. The
Violin and Piano Sonata (1937) though grim and intense,
is one of his most direct and easily approachable. The
lucidity of the church works here finds a masterly con-
certante expression. In the Introduction and Andante the
basis is a firm diatonic C minor with polytonal intrusions.
The violin line is passionately lyrical, a development of
the Bach and Buxtehude baroque, and the music proceeds
by remorselessly logical extensions of the opening figures
to a tremendous climax achieved by progressively expanding leaps in the fioritura and by increasingly anguished
unresolved appoggiaturas :

The allegretto movement which follows is in Wellesz's glittering, almost Hindemithian, but completely personal, moto perpetuo manner, and again preserves a diatonic foundation. The work as a whole is magnificently exciting to play and shows how the greatest lyrical vitality is always inseparable from severe formal discipline.

The String Quartet, op. 60, I am inclined to think the finest of Wellesz's chamber works. The first movement, intensely dramatic, opens with one of Wellesz's vigorous, sinewy unison passages in free tonal extensions around G minor :

A subsidiary tranquil drooping figure appears contrapuntally shortly before the statement of the second subject-group in bouncing persistent rhythm, with many glinting sevenths and ninths, beautifully laid out for the medium. The inter-operation of this widely contrasted material is managed with superb economy. The end, with violins and viola singing a modification of the drooping figure over the 'cello's ostinato-like statement of the first theme, attains to a classic inevitability :

The Scherzo, a sprightly, free twelve-note piece in which the row gives considerable prominence to diatonic triads, is at once jaunty and wistful, instrumental and lyrical—a typically ambivalent quality of Wellesz's writing in this vein. Again the texture has economy and grace. The climax of the work comes in the concluding slow movement, a magnificent piece of melodic writing with long lines of great span, genuinely instrumental in quality but warmly lyrical, alternating with a passage in quietly persistent syncopated rhythm. The opening is a particularly fine example of Wellesz's method of achieving intensity by treating apparently atonal progressions as unresolved suspensions and appoggiaturas over a tonal foundation ; the tonality of G minor is implicit throughout the passage but never directly stated :

The music develops by passionate arabesques in the various parts, with increasing extensions of the intervals, again a more extreme application of the technique in late Mahler. The close is luminous and remote, the quiet syncopated figure in violins and viola, the lyrical theme gradually disintegrating in the 'cello. This is music which though related to the early chamber works, could never have been written but for the experience of the music dramas and the discipline of the liturgical works.

This religious quality is prominent too in Wellesz's next work, a setting of Hopkin's *The Leaden and the Golden Echo* for soprano, violin, clarinet, 'cello and piano. Hopkin's poem, Shakespearian in its contact with the spoken language, baroque in its virtuoso qualities, has obvious affinities both with Wellesz's technical methods and with his ethical preoccupations. The setting marks the lifting of the 'nervous' impressionism of his early years into an impersonal religious apprehension of innocence and experience. The same pliant tonal and rhythmic speech inflection in the vocal line, the same glittering, shimmering arabesque in the instrumental parts, but now realized with classical objectivity; again a very free use is made of a twelve note row embodying a diatonic triad :

O.___ is there no frown-ing of those wrink-les, rank-èd

wrink-les deep   down ?

The tremulous glowing texture is unique, extremely
beautiful, and apposite to the yearning innocence of
Hopkin's poem. The use of the C major harmonies at
the opening of the *Golden Echo,* after the confused con-
torted lines of the despair passage, attains the maximum of
poignancy with the minimum of means. It is testimony to
the maturity of a great artist.

The purity of technique and emotion which we find
in the *Echo* cantata is manifested much more simply in
the two little choral pieces for women's voices, settings
of the mediaeval carol *I sing of a maiden,* and of Fletcher's
song *See the day begins to break.* The idiom of these, however, has no connection with Wellesz's Schönbergian origins
but rather with some aspects of the re-creation of mediaeval
vocal technique which we find in the works of his 'liturgical' period. (Note, for instance, the use of parallel seconds
in the carol). In their different way these songs are no less
remarkable than the Hopkins cantata for the sensitivity
they show to the English language ; there would seem to be
something in the spirit of the early English poetry which
corresponds closely to an aspect of Wellesz's sensibility.

Up to this point, Wellesz had not produced in England
any work on a scale comparable with the operas written
in his native country. In 1945, however, he composed a
full-scale symphony which must take its place among his
most important creations. It is significant that he, who
had always been primarily an opera composer, should
have produced his first symphony late in life ; and that
this symphony should impress one both as a completely
'contemporary' work and as one which has the weight of
tradition behind it. It looked as though the Viennese
symphonic line of Haydn, Mozart, Schubert, Bruckner and
Mahler had come to an end in the elegiac last movement
of Mahler's Ninth ; and as we have seen it is certainly
true that in so far as the composers of the Schönberg
group (including Wellesz in his earlier days) carried on
from Mahler's Ninth, they tended to develop techniques

suggested by that work which were not essentially symphonic. But in 1945 Wellesz has proved that the Viennese symphony is after all not a back-number, that it is still capable of growth.

Broadly speaking he re-creates the Viennese symphony by mating the technique of late Mahler with the Bachian-baroque aspects of his own idiom which we have already referred to in connection with the Violin Sonata; so that we may perhaps say that the Symphony is the consummation of the main line of his development since the *Bacchantes*. The first movement is conceived on a vast scale; after a slow introduction this massively energetic theme is stated and developed with considerable intensity in the dissonant part-writing of the inner lines; here, as throughout the work, the orchestration is lucidly linear in conception:

As in the Violin Sonata the polytonal elements and incidental dissonances are 'baroque' intensifications of a stable tonal conception rooted in Bach and Buxtehude: (the Symphony is unambiguously described as being in C minor). The second subject is suaver and more lyrical, developing some of the triplet figurations of the counterpoints to the first subject. The development section proper is elaborate and extensive, incorporating a fully evolved fugue, remarkable for the exciting dissonant clashes of its closely wrought sequential writing. The recapitulation is orthodox, with the second subject reappearing in E flat instead of the initial B flat. This tremendous movement concludes with a long muscular stretto over a dominant pedal, and a coda re-statement of the main theme in the major, with all its original polytonal complexities resolved into unequivocal diatonicism. At the very end a triumphant version of a characteristic rhythm of the introduction is powerfully reiterated.

The Scherzo is a strange unearthly piece built over a quintuplet moto perpetuo. The orchestration has a peculiar luminosity, particularly in the trio with its tenuous texture and abrupt groupings of unrelated triads:

The last movement—an adagio—like the last movement of Mahler's Ninth—explicitly relates the Bachian baroque elements of Wellesz's work to Mahler. It opens with a noble Mahlerian rhetorical phrase for solo strings; but the 'pathetic' rhetoric is always disciplined by an austerity that relates both to the Bachian baroque and to liturgical elements of mediaeval music (see, for instance, the sombre homophonic interlude). The atmosphere is of a Mahler still more radiant and rarefied:

The end of the work, though it is certainly no mere imitation but authentic re-creation, invites comparison with the famous 'dissolving' end of Mahler's *Das Lied von der Erde*.

Since the Symphony Wellesz has composed two settings

of Dryden and Milton for baritone and piano. These songs
reaffirm the manner of the Symphony; the melting, pentatonic end of 'Ah Fading Joy' may be compared with
the end of the Symphony, and the energetic rhythm and
muscular linear texture of the Milton song may be
correlated with the Symphony's first movement. The vocal
line may be regarded as a modification of the virtuoso
tradition of Purcell (note the baroque flourishes on the
'expressive' words), reconciled with the composer's Austrian
and European heritage. Like the Hopkins cantata, these
songs provide evidence, if evidence were needed, that
Wellesz could now write an opera surpassing in positive
assurance, tenderness and power, even his splendid earlier
achievement. Let us hope that as part of the much vaunted
re-birth of opera in England we shall tardily honour the
one great exiled European composer we have amongst us,
as the Americans have rather surprisingly honoured
Schönberg, Hindemith, Bartók, Milhaud, and Stravinsky.
In any case, to the chamber works there can be no objections on economic grounds. It is time that they were
performed.

—Counterpoint, 1945.

VIII

KODALY AND THE
CHRISTIAN EPIC

THAT CENTRAL EUROPE SHOULD have produced
three out of the dozen (generously speaking) twentieth-
century composers who have outstandingly original genius
is not as surprising as might superficially appear. Janácek,
Bartók and Kodály possess various distinctive traits of
sensibility which we may properly call contemporary ; yet
they all derive something of their power from the fact
that they were nurtured in countries in which a tradition
of popular music was still a living actuality, rather than a
matter for antiquarian research. Janácek and Bartók left
the folk idiom far behind—Janácek in his increasingly personal rhythmically complex idiom based on the flexibilities
of speech, Bartók in his elaboration of a technique derived
first from a rhythmic conception of dissonance and later
from an extension of the eighteenth-century melodic conception, combined with a feeling for the line-drawing of
Asiatic music. But for all their originality, their nervous
intensity, their isolation—all the qualities we sum up as
their contemporaneity—one feels that they could not have
been composers of so urgent a purpose if they had not
profited by a unique combination of circumstances. However personal their idiom, their impetus for creation came
from a source that was at once deeper and more far-
reaching.

Of the three composers Kodály is undoubtedly the
smallest and the simplest. In his work contemporaneity
of sensibility has not often sought a violent outlet, but is
implicit in a certain meditative introspection, a turning-
inwards which is nostalgic in origin ; so that one is not

surprised to discover that his *harmonic* idiom, with its tranquil sevenths and ninths, has some kinship with that of Debussy. But his introspection is saved from over-subjectivity by the traditional folk-sense that gives to his melodies a distinctive ripeness and soaring plasticity of contour. His melody, a natural utterance of the human singing voice, with its rhythms and inflexions moulded by the Hungarian language, has therefore much of the modal suppleness of folk-song, often with a pentatonic foundation; and it may be examined in its simplest and perhaps most satisfying form in his early songs Op. 6 and Op. 14, particularly the 'Fragment of a Letter to a Friend'. The lines are passionately direct and, despite the sophistication of the comparatively static (Debussyan) harmonic accompaniment, almost naïve; but although they do not attempt to express obscure or difficult states of feeling their lyrical sweep is so lithe and warm and human that it is like a significant bodily movement, tender and intense as a woman nursing her child. These songs seem to me some of the most beautiful vocal music of our time, and they contain the essence of Kodály's talent. All his representative work is vocally and lyrically conceived; in the instrumental works, particularly the piano pieces and string quartets, the folky inflexions tend to degenerate into perfunctory and unconvincing rhapsody, the sevenths and ninths to become precious in a sense that is almost dilettante.

Depending as it does on this compromise between the spontaneous nostalgia of the vocal and 'modal' lyricism of folk speech, and the comparative sophistication of a harmonic dialect, Kodály's music is necessarily limited in scope: he cannot, like Bartók, hope to create a technique which may play a part in the evolution of European music in the future. But it is not by any means limited to successes of the type defined by the early songs, and perhaps his most important works are those which, similarly conceived in a vocal and lyrical manner, and equally

direct in their sensibility, are executed in more epic proportions, being associated with the native, 'popular' aspects
of the Christian religion. Such works are the *Psalmus
Hungaricus* and the *Budavári Te Deum*. The first has been
several times performed in this country and is recognized
as a masterpiece; the second is little known and, with
reference to the case I have been making out about
Kodály's representative significance, perhaps more interesting. This is why I want to consider it in some detail.

Conceived for soloists, chorus and full orchestra, the
Te Deum opens with an imposing fanfare and a kind of
rhetorical introduction in which the choir participates. The
basis of the method is exemplified in the 'tibi omnes'
section :

or later

where the extremely simple harmonic scheme is derived
from lines moulded in terms of the human voice, producing
a procession of *harmonically* unrelated concords similar
to that of the more chromatic writing of the sixteenth century. Although Kodály modifies this technique
to the extent of introducing occasionally his characteristic
sevenths and ninths, the method remains the same; it is
merely that these chords have become part of his stock
of concords. Kodály's harmonies in his big vocal works

are never esoteric in effect but simple in accordance with the soaring sweep of the lines. This is particularly noticeable in the insistence on the dominant ninth during the building-up of the big climax, achieved by a beautifully suave movement in the parts, which concludes the first section on the word 'Sabaoth'; and such melodic and harmonic traits are the technical representation of Kodály's sanguine blend of sweetness with virility.

Then follows, at 'Pleni sunt coeli', a fugue on this vigorous subject :

in which the important interval is the rising or falling fourth. The first and second violins interject a more agile version of the theme, treated in free canon ; and the tonal feeling, with the transitions still very flexible, might be said to tend towards a transposed Dorian. (The distrust of the leading note is typical of almost all Kodály's music). After a big climax based on an augmentation of the rising fourth motif, the fugue merges at 'Te martyrum' into a section which alternates between tranquil homophonic vocal periods in Kodály's personal modification of the sixteenth-century idiom and another vigorous quasi-pentatonic orchestral theme built on rising fourths, combined with reminiscences of the opening fanfare :

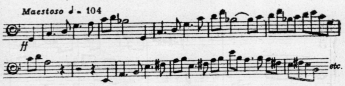

A sweetly lucid passage at 'Venerandum tuum', making a representative 'static' use of the augmented sixth, then leads into an adagio setting of the 'Tu rex gloriae', the melodic material of which evolves out of the last vigorous passage on rising fourths. In this section the rhythmic flexibility, the exquisite interflow of the parts, the delicacy of the orchestral harmonies underlying with their tranquil sevenths the growth of the voices, assume at once their most lucid and their most subtle form. The mould of the lines has here a pronounced pentatonic feeling and is obviously affiliated, both tonally and rhythmically, with folk-song :

From this 'speaking' lyricism the polyphonic **texture** grows until a powerful climax is built up by way of the orchestra's characteristic insistence on the chord of the ninth. Except for a brief reference to the movement of the opening allegro this section is developed on a large scale over the dotted rhythm enunciated by the strings until it dissolves, at 'Te ergo quaesumus', in a mysterious tremolo.

A fine swinging theme enters at 'in gloria' and is soon inter-linked with an extension of the rising fourth theme. This merges at 'per singulos dies' into a big recapitulation of the opening fanfare combined with a modification of the dotted rhythm of the adagio. 'In te Domine' is an elaborate double fugue, the voices developing this superbly conceived vocal subject :

and the strings this equally string-like one :

The tonality—a very free transposed Lydian—and the rhythmic structure are again closer to the sixteenth century than to the principles of Handelian counterpoint, and a vigorous use is made of the rising fifth which seems to compensate the falling fourth which is so prominent at the beginning of the first fugue-subject.

Intermingled with the 'in te Domine' themes, the subject of this first fugue re-appears at 'non confundar', and leads to a development of the words 'in aeternam', based on the soaring fourths in increasingly concentrated stretto, an extremely poignant effect being achieved by the anguished suspensions on the top note of the phrase which then droops in pathetic chromaticism (note too the intensity of the chromatic alteration creating the augmented instead of the perfect fourth):

etc.

The final climax is founded on an augmentation of the fourths motif and a recapitulation of the opening fanfare: there is a brief and exquisite coda with a typical chromatic intrusion in a harmony of diatonic concords.

What makes the *Te Deum* so remarkable a composition is, I am inclined to think, its polyphonic texture which implies a clarification and in a sense a deepening of Kodály's emotional processes. In the largely homophonic *Psalmus Hungaricus* Kodály seemed to have expressed consummately all that he had to say in his direct folk-founded technique, and it seemed to me unlikely that he could develop further along those lines. He would either have to stop composing, or to repeat himself, or to become relatively factitious, or to evolve a new manner. In view of the specialized nature of his musical upbringing the last of these alternatives seemed improbable, and many of the later choral works, not to mention the instrumental ones, did seem to betray a disturbingly synthetic quality. But in the *Budavári Te Deum* Kodály, without sacrificing any of the spontaneity and passionate simplicity of his mode of experience, incarnates it in a polyphonic technique of surprising flexibility and power, and in so doing presents to us the essence of this experience with a lucidity and a depth that he had not, in the magnificently vital songs and the *Psalmus Hungaricus,* quite approached. The experience is not fundamentally more difficult or 'profound', but its implications are more exhaustively realized. Its simplicity, more so even than the simplicity of the songs, is here its strength, and it is a serene simplicity such as we shall look for in vain in almost all other contemporary music of anything approaching a comparable power. The earlier music of Vaughan Williams—to cite a local example that would appear to be broadly parallel— has none of Kodály's spontaneity because Vaughan Williams's achievement in an urbanized community inevitably betrayed a degree of self-consciousness that Kodály had less need of. Perhaps Kodály's significance in cultural history is more comparable with the position occupied in English literature by T. F. Powys; in any case the accomplishment was a precarious one which once done cannot be repeated. What Busoni said of Tirso de Molina's *Don Juan Tenorio* might apply also to Kodály's *Te Deum* : 'It is powerful, has great freshness and facility, is big, and at the same time naïve'. And in a sense it would be apposite to continue the quotation and to add : 'The creative artist will never reach this point again. The time for unaffectedness is past, and we reckon with too large a public that knows too much about a variety of things'. Although Kodály may compose other music as good as the *Te Deum,* I doubt if he will write any better ; and I am certain that he will have no successors. Because of, rather than in spite of, his technical fluency in the *Budavári Te Deum* he is, in the history of European music, the last great naïf.

—*Music and Letters,* 1941.

IX

HOLST AND THE ENGLISH LANGUAGE

AN AMIABLE PERSONALITY, NOT himself an unusually passionate man, Holst has excited more violent passions than any other contemporary English composer. How difficult he is to assess as a creative artist is perhaps indicated by the extraordinary fluctuations in his reputation. For years he was completely ignored; after *The Planets* and the *Ode to Death* had seen him larded with an adulation that proved acutely embarrassing to him he was for some time the unwilling recipient of national and even international honours; and then the flame petered out as suddenly as it had kindled, and the later works were received with callous frigidity. He has never recovered his earlier glory—which was, as we shall see, something like a sport in the career of a composer whose genius is inherently forbidding—and his most representative works are now seldom performed. But if one feels that there are qualifications to be made about the nature of his genius— even if one feels that scarcely one of his works is altogether successful and completely realized—it is these qualifications which give him his unique historical significance; and perhaps it is sufficient to add that genius seems the right word.

Only as a teacher is Holst's reputation untarnished, and the work which he did at St. Paul's School and at Morley College, performing sixteenth and twentieth-century English music (in particular Byrd, Weelkes and Vaughan Williams), has exerted an influence down to the present day; while at the Royal College he proved an inspiring figure in his insistence at once on contrapuntal discipline and on true creative freedom, based on absolute economy of means. Yet as a composer his relation to the English sixteenth century is a somewhat curious one, for he is not, like his pupil Edmund Rubbra, directly a lyrical and polyphonic composer. His knowledge and love of English Tudor music rather conditioned his peculiar approach to his art, and this approach came to be centred in the relationship between his music and the English language.

When we speak of the relation between music and language we mean one of two things. We may mean the way in which a musical language is as it were sub-consciously moulded by the verbal language its creator speaks and has been familiar with since his earliest childhood—the way in which the lines of Purcell are recognizably English or those of Fauré representatively French. Or we may mean the more particular connection between music and a specific verbal text—a problem allied but distinct—where the basic difficulty is to reconcile a precise concern for the articulation of the verbal phrase with the evolution of a self-subsistent lyrical line. We can most simply examine both relationships in folk-songs, the most 'direct' form of musical art, in that the folk-idiom is moulded by the language and yet is so musical and lyrical as to be perfectly satisfying if sung without words. Thus although in the one sense a great lyrical music may be said not only to start from, but also to sublimate, an interest in the accentuation of the words, it would appear that in another sense there is a certain antipathy between the singing voice and speech, so that the perfect solutions of the problem are few and far between. In English song one can point to Dowland, Purcell and Warlock's *The Curlew* as representative examples.

Now Holst started from a concern for an English musical utterance such as is implied in the English language. 'I find that *unconsciously* I have been drawn for years', he said, 'towards discovering the (or a) musical idiom of the English language. Never having managed to learn a foreign language, songs had always meant for me a peg of words on which to hang a tune. The great awakening came on hearing the recitatives in Purcell's *Dido.*' It seems to me that in this preoccupation with the relation between English music and the English language is the real significance of his interest in the English folk-song movement. It is true that, as he used to say, he had been brought up to believe that folk-songs were 'either bad or Irish', and that the work of Cecil Sharp was a revelation to him; but it was not a revelation in the sense that it entailed any re-creation of vanished glory. Holst did not see in the folk-song cult any wistful reversion to a simpler, more 'primitive' form of existence; he admired the songs' simplicity and economy, their emotional beauty combined with impersonality, but most of all he was interested in them because words and tune had grown up together. In folk-song he could see how 'primitive' English composers—indeed the English folk—had set about the evolution of an English musical language. His own melodic idiom has affinities with that of English folk-song because he was obsessed with the same problem; he used modal tonalities, pentatonic linear formulæ, because that is the way in which English people spontaneously sing, the deepest root of the musical language in the verbal one. Most of the difficulty of his melodic idiom comes from the fact that, completely unsentimental, it arouses expectations which it does not fulfil. He adopts these traits in a personal manner, and those who expect the easy folk-mongering appeal because his melodic technique appears to start from the implications of folk-song are doomed to disappointment.

One of his *Four Mediaeval Lyrics* for voice and violin offers an excellent opportunity for examining the basis of his melodic speech :

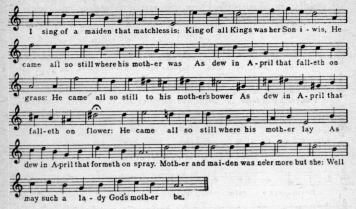

I sing of a maiden that matchless is: King of all Kings was her Son i - wis, He came all so still where his moth-er was As dew in A - pril that fall-eth on grass: He came all so still to his moth-er's bower As dew in A - pril that fall-eth on flower: He came all so still where his moth-er lay As dew in A-pril that formeth on spray. Moth-er and mai-den was ne'er more but she: Well may such a la - dy God's moth-er be.

This is perhaps as close as Holst came to folk-song, and we can observe how the intimate relation between voice and verse is reconciled with the problem of structural balance by the comparatively naïve, .folk-song-like device of repetition. But we can also observe, in the middle section, a personal twist to the folky tonality which gives intimation of how, when a more sophisticated text and medium are in question, Holst's solution of the problem becomes likewise more complicated; and this solution lies, I would say, half-way between the speaking voice as declamation, and song.

The essence of declamation is that in deference to the exigencies of speech it eschews the long lyrical phrase and becomes relatively fragmentary. Now Holst does sublimate speech into a phrase of some considerable extent but not to the pitch of song; he sublimates speech to a sustained *prose* rhythm rather than to the contour of lyricism. The following quotations will illustrate his mature melodic style, and we can see from them that the link with folk-song still prevails—in, for instance, the pentatonic feeling of parts of the latter two. But it is clear too that both the rhythmic plasticity and the tonality have acquired a subdued wavering instability which gives to the line its coldly desolate effect—a mournful frigidity in which is contained, perhaps, the essence of Holst's contribution:

This is a very specialized idiom and we may say that Holst is not a great lyricist, which explains why he is not among the great composers of history. But his unique position, his oddity as a cultural phenomenon, consists precisely in his allowing the prose phrase integral expression without trying to emotionalize it or to compensate *for* it with a sensuous harmonic vocabulary.

His early works, it is true, were comparatively elaborate and chromatic in harmony (he described them as 'good old Wagnerian bawling'), but his development manifests a gradual purging. *The Planets, The Perfect Fool,* and to some extent the *Ode to Death* are important as transitional works in that in them one can observe a conventional nineteenth-century harmonic background merging into the irregular and abrupt Holstian prose rhythms and the characteristic modal structures. (Their enormous popularity can perhaps be traced to the fact that they were to contemporary audiences superficially startling without being fundamentally disturbing to emotional complacency.) Just as Roussel arrived at a basically French idiom by way of researches into oriental music, so Holst's search for an English idiom was facilitated by his researches, in the *Rig Veda* and other works, into the modal *melodic* idioms of non-European musics ; and he came more and more to think of his harmonies in a prose sense too—to make them extensions of the prose melodic lines. Because the linear conception is a prose one it follows that Holst does not attempt the reconciliation of the horizontal with the vertical that is the supreme technical achievement of the sixteenth century, but rather writes according to principles analogous to those of pre-sixteenth-century music. There is a prevalence of unison writing ; and a number of the harmonic effects—even some of the most 'daring' ones—turn out to be merely an extension of the unison principle to parallel fourths and triads, as in organum, with the difference that more than one such 'thickened out' part may be in motion at the same time. What is often referred to as his 'fondness for the six-four chord' is thus hardly a harmonic device at all ; it is merely a thickening of the melodic writing which helps to create the bareness and austerity typical of the emotional temper of his most characteristic work ; for instance, this passage from the *Choral Fantasia :*

Sometimes the economy is carried to the extreme of the thickening of a unison line over a pedal. The opening of the First Choral Symphony and most of the part song *Say Who is This* (from op. 44) are powerful examples; and the notorious clash of an F sharp major six-four with an F major six-four in a choral passage of the *Hymn of Jesus* is as logically explicable melodically as are the false relations of the sixteenth century.

Another way of considering Holst's interior pedals—and also his fondness for ground basses—is to regard them as the result of a sub-conscious desire to compensate for the rhythmic implications of the prose melody; for so extreme a rhythmic freedom, if it is not sublimated into lyricism, makes the problem of formal integration increasingly difficult. However this may be, internal pedals and ground basses are often used—in *Egdon Heath* and the *Hymn of Jesus* for instance—to provide anchorage for the wavering prose lines, and the tension between the two is another of the means whereby is generated the music's somewhat agonized intensity.

All these characteristics are most notable in the choral works, to which they are obviously most pertinent. In a few late works, such as the *Fugal Overture* and *Fugal Concerto,* and the Concerto for two violins, Holst seems consciously to be working out an 'instrumental' technique, combining his harmonic austerity with a more regular metrical sense in the manner of the lesser instrumental works of Bach rather than in the flexible rhythms of sixteenth-century counterpoint. Folk-song still symbolizes the element of vocal utterance ; the Bachian element his mastery of purely instrumental form ; and the two aspects are combined but never reconciled. The vocal and instrumental aspects seem to correspond to two emotional manners, a piteous melancholy of vocal prose rhythm and a mode of dynamic metrical ferocity. It is because the music is so honest that its quality of bareness and economy is so oddly disturbing ; if anything is meant by calling Holst a 'mystic' it can only be that of all musical idioms his became among the least sensual.

Of these late works the finest is the *Scherzo,* which was all he wrote of a projected Symphony. Here the modes of doleful, wailing vocal prose-rhythm and brusque metrical violence are juxtaposed with an intensity which Holst had never before approached ; and Vaughan Williams's Fourth Symphony indicates how this intensity exerted an influence even on so vigorous a personality, though the comparable parts of this work are relatively crude and quite without the uniquely strange poignancy of Holst's music. It almost seems that this poignancy comes from the very integrity of the music's *failure* to reconcile disparate emotional climates, just as Holst's importance as a representative figure lies in his honest pre-occupation with, rather than in his solution of, the pro-blems which English composers are obliged to tackle. He was, indeed, one of the first to teach English composers of the twentieth century what these fundamental problems were : and one cannot say, of a composer whose virtues are so peculiarly inter-linked with his limitations, that he would have been a better artist if he had 'achieved serenity' ; even though he would certainly have been a different one. *Egdon Heath* and the *Scherzo*—his two masterpieces and, apart from a few very impressive but slight things such as the songs for voice and violin, pro-bably his only unqualified successes—are both compositions of a pervasive melancholy and spiritual unrest. In considering his final position one cannot, I think, do better than to close with Imogen Holst's account of his reaction to a performance of the Schubert Quintet : 'As he listened to Schubert's Quintet he realized what he had lost, not only in his music but in his life. He could cling to his austerity. He could fill his days with kindness and good-humour. He could write music that was neither common-place, unmeaning, nor tame . . . But he missed the warmth of the Schubert Quintet. At the moment, it seemed as if this warmth were the only thing worth having'.

If one adds to this that he resembled Weelkes, whom he so much admired, in his inventive originality and English unexpectedness while lacking Weelkes's lyrical rich-ness and geniality, it will be with no pejorative implica-tion : for the Tudor composer's warmth, and Holst's frigidity, bear testimony to the remoteness, in more than time, of two cultural worlds.

Music Review 1941.

X

RUBBRA AND THE DOMINANT SEVENTH:

Notes on an English Symphony

'We want, not a new technique, but the old feeling, felt as new.'—W. B. YEATS.

I

IT WAS THE CUSTOM of the late Donald Francis Tovey to divide musical composition into two main classes, which he called, respectively, musical textures and musical shapes. The prime example of the musical texture is the fugue, and all music in the broadest sense fugally conceived : the prime example of the musical shape or architecture is the classical diatonic symphony or sonata. The musical texture is associated, roughly speaking, with melody and the voice, is fluid in tonality and rhythm, is continuous, polyphonic and self-generative, and has no 'form' apart from the organic evolution of its component lines. The shape, on the other hand, with its double bars and repeats, its exposition, development and recapitulation, its opposition of 'subjects' and key-centres, is homophonic rather than polyphonic, dance-like rather than vocal, and has a clearly defined architectural symmetry which may (if only for convenience) be mentally imaged apart from the evolution of the lines, as the physical movements of a dance exist apart from the dance's music. The texture or fugue attains the utmost emotional tension within the conventions of melodic language ; the contrasts of key-centres which are the mainstay of the diatonic sonata imbue it with a quality to which we apply, perhaps clumsily, the adjective 'dramatic'. Thus there is a popularly accepted notion that it is possible to consider a Beethoven (or even a Mozart) symphonic movement as a kind of microcosm of a human drama, not to mention the crudities to which such an approach is susceptible with, say, Tchaikowsky. Of course the notion is fundamentally fallacious since no music, as distinct from ideas *about* music, can be apprehended except through the human ear; but perhaps we may legitimately say that there is less likelihood of our attempting to apprehend fugal or texture music in other than musical terms.

One cannot imagine a Bach fugue or a Palestrina motet requiring any purely architectural chords to complete it; on the other hand the forty odd bars of the chord of C major at the end of Beethoven's Fifth Symphony do not contain a single redundancy; such is the nature of the texture-shape distinction[1]. Of course this is inevitably a crude re-statement of Tovey's case, and there can be no hard and fast line, for in any healthy musical society textures and shapes are inter-operative, mutually enriching each other (for instance, most of Bach's dance movements and arias, the concerted arias of Mozart, the finale of the 'Jupiter'). None the less, I think it may be accepted that a decay of the principles of texture is a decay of the fundamentals of musical speech, and that a musical architecture is likely to collapse if it has no foundation other than rhythm and harmony divorced from melody, polyphony and the voice. The 'rules' of harmony itself enforce this contention; and certainly at the beginning of the present century the prevailing homophony was so far enfeebled (the sociological-cum-technical reasons for this prevalence do not concern us here) that the more significant com-

1 *Cf.* Schweitzer's *Bach,* Vol. 1, p. 211: 'Bach's way of working, as Spitta says, was quite different from Beethoven's. The latter experimented with his thoughts. In each case the explanation must be sought in the nature of the music itself. With Beethoven the work is developed by means of "episodes" that are independent of the theme. These do not occur in Bach; with him everything that "happens" is simply an emanation from the theme.'

posers almost without exception felt imperative the re-creation of texture and a vocal mode of thought.

For some time it seemed as though the symphony was doomed, being essentially a product of diatonicism, and hence of an age more stable than our own. In Mahler's Ninth Symphony one can see the diatonic symphony dis-integrating into a very beautiful twilight which presages atonalism and the twelve-tone instrumental texture ; and although Sibelius gave the symphony fresh vigour it has always seemed to me that (except possibly in No. 4) he is the last of the old diatonic-homophonic ethos, rather than the beginning of something new. After Sibelius, the com-poser who has made the most significant and *consistent* contribution to the contemporary symphonic problem is Edmund Rubbra, and technically one can say that he has worked towards making free polyphonic lines the basis of symphonic structure ; or towards the reconciliation of tex-ture and shape. The symphonic problem, as Rubbra conceives it, is probably the central problem of musical evolution to-day.

I have written elsewhere[2] of what I take to be the importance of Rubbra's first three symphonies. Here it is necessary to say of them only that the remorselessness of the free polyphony developed over the whole orchestra, and on symphonic dimensions, gives to the first two an extreme nervous intensity that may properly be called contemporary, though both works are of a bigness, serious-ness and originality besides which much contemporary music looks like child's play (the slow movement of No. 2, Rubbra's finest achievement up to that date, is, however, also his most 'classical' and profoundly calm). The much greater clarity and *apparent* simplicity of No. 3 is testi-mony both to the maturity of the composer's spiritual resources and to his more completely successful solution of his symphonic problem of the reconciliation of texture and shape—the 'spiritual' and 'technical' are, of course,

2   See *Music and Society.*

ultimately identical. No. 3 is more lucid, more clearly organized, more stable in tonality and at the same time more vocal, more lyrical, more fluid. It is perhaps the most 'positive' work in twentieth-century music; and it is a perfect reconciliation of the principles of texture with those of shape. No. 4 is no less positive, perhaps even warmer and richer, but also subtler, more delicate, at once tender and strong in sensibility. I want to approach this characteristic subtlety by way of a technical feature which is not very noticeable in Rubbra's earlier work—I mean his treatment of the dominant seventh.

II

The unprepared dominant seventh, the history books tell us, not altogether accurately, was the chord with which Monteverdi revolutionized musical history; the chord most closely associated with the dominant-tonic cadence of the architecture of the classical symphony and with the sequence of romanticism—a chord of finality and symmetry, or of harmonic chromaticism, to which Rubbra's idiom, with its vocal lyricism, its prevalence of conjunct motion and perfect consonances, its plastic modality and rhythm, its transitions rather than modulations, its insistence on continuity and melodic generation, is severely opposed. So close, indeed, is Rubbra's melodic idiom and his principle of melodic-polyphonic growth to the methods of the sixteenth century, for all his originality, that his symphonies have been referred to, excusably if inadequately, as gigantic instrumental motets; and it is not surprising that in music so texturally conceived the dominant seventh should have little place[3]. In the harsh and austere 1st, and the polyphonically very complex 2nd the harmonic subtlety depends largely on polyphonic treatment of the triad: in No. 3 the dominant seventh appears more frequently but in a fluid and usually

---

3 Rubbra's teacher Holst developed an almost fanatical hatred of the dominant seventh; though I do not think this 'influence' was the fundamental reason for Rubbra's distrust of the chord.

melodic guise. The harmony of No. 4 again shows no trace of the higher chromatic discords, and apart from polyphonic combinations includes only diatonic triads and seventh chords. But these seventh chords have now become a prominent part of the harmonic idiom, appearing many times homophonically; and the fact that the chord has been absorbed into Rubbra's 'generative' lyric symphony testifies to an expansion of his technique (a still wider acceptance of homophony within a basically polyphonic idiom) which in turn reflects a deepening quality of experience.

The originality of Rubbra's use of the dominant seventh is another instance of his power to create a personal and self-consistent idiom out of the accepted materials of European tradition, without indulgence in the explicitly revolutionary. In Rubbra's Fourth the dominant seventh has all its traditional warmth and full-bloodedness but none of its conventional penultimate implications. The sevenths do not 'resolve': like his tonal and rhythmic sense they are lucid but continually flowing, so that they acquire, in their lyric context, a quality at once rich and curiously pure and disembodied. A traditional material of homophony and of musical shape here merges into texture; and the increased warmth and serenity of No. 4 might be said to be summarized in this insistence on the dominant seventh, while the increased subtlety and poignancy is summarized in the textural manner in which this insistence is made.

The spacious homophonic opening of the first movement (*con moto*) is an excellent example of this, besides illustrating the characteristic fluidity of the always beautifully singable tonal sense :

Despite this homophony, the movement has no 'external' architecture. The generation is entirely lyrical—the continuous growth of melodic ideas into fresh organisms, sometimes by the gradual extension of a phrase, sometimes by the dissection of a phrase into its component parts. These components, after the generation of the new idea, may continue to fulfil a subservient function in the contrapuntal texture. Almost all the melodic material of the movement springs from the falling fifth and rising third (both major and minor) of the opening phrase; the throbbing syncopated undercurrent of dominant sevenths and diatonic concords—continually oscillating to and from the seventh which never resolves—gives to the evolution of the lyricism a warmth which is also quietly expectant, instinct with intimations of new germination and eventual blossoming. Soon, indeed, a little curling semi-quaver figure (*cf.* the semi-tonal figure which plays so important a part in No. 3) emerges from some cross-bar extensions of the line, increasingly to dominate the whole movement. For the first time a key-centre (E minor) is established when this figure is developed in a rich passage of dialogue between horns and low strings, though the lines remain always plastic, finely lyrical and vocal in feeling. The tonality relaxes again while the semi-quaver figure continues incessantly and the phrases of falling fifths

and rising thirds become more and more subtly inter-
woven. After an exquisitely tender passage on falling fifths
there eventually generates a ferocious extension of the
rising third phrase on the trombones. This leads, by
way of a supple swaying sequential passage on strings
(harmonically founded on dominant sevenths and developing the more animated trombone rhythm), to the building
up of a big climax over the semi-quaver figure's dynamic
pulse, the harmonies oscillating between dominant sevenths
of D and B. The passage from the trombone melody to
the build-up of the climax may be quoted as a particularly
beautiful and typical example of Rubbra's method :

Over this base a fresh theme, the nearest approach to an orthodox 'second subject', generates itself on the wood-wind, from the syncopated rhythm and dominant sevenths of the opening accompaniment :

During the 'meno mosso' passage a fluid G minor had established itself and intimations of a 'modal' C minor and F minor are heard as a flowing song-like counter-subject in triplets grows on the strings through the mingling of conjunct motion with the rising thirds and falling fifths. The texture becomes increasingly poly-phonic as the music gathers momentum over a timpani pedal on A flat, and the movement's climax comes (with a G minorish return) in a medley of the independent rhythms of the various melodies, horns and brass inter-jecting aggressive diminutions and double diminutions of the 'second subject' figure. Every strand of the tissue of this climax, the only 'dissonant' passage in the whole movement, is a consequence of logical polyphonic growth ; even in this extreme passage one can observe (though, of course, it is a matter of experience and not of theory) the seed of the flowing string melody in the original rising third and falling fifth :

The tension calms and leads, not to a conventional recapitulation, but to a section resembling the homophonic opening, though with the tonal relations, beginning in E flat major-minor, still more compressed and elliptical. The tonality finally droops down to D major (D being significantly the flat seventh from the opening E), with the curling semi-quaver figure insisting on the flattened seventh, thereby at the close consummating melodically what remains to the end harmonically unresolved. If it is possible to give any technical explanation of the profound calm of the close of this movement, the most serene music Rubbra has given us, I think it must be in terms of the melodic significance with which the composer invests, at this point, the flattened seventh; and perhaps in terms of the explicit statement, by the woodwind, in the closing bars, of the previously implicit relation between the 'second subject' and the opening syncopated accompaniment.

Dominant sevenths do not pervade the other movements to the same extent, but appear frequently in the flowing texture of the second, an Intermezzo. Whereas the first movement generates melody and climax with the utmost intensity, the Intermezzo glides by without climax, and is rather a series of uninterrupted reflections on a single melody-group which the polyphony kaleidoscopically presents in shifting tonal and rhythmic guises. (This polyphonic commentary rather than growth has been used in the scherzo of No. 3 also.) The movement's main melodic material is indicated in the following quotation :

and its light, continuous play of fancy, in a delicate waltz rhythm, serves as a brief, gentle relaxation between the concentration of the first movement and the third. Particularly remarkable is the manner in which the subtlety of the linear contour fully reveals only when the parts are allotted their orchestral tone-colour, exquisitely soft and pearly, dominated by violas and wood-wind, with an occasional piquancy of trumpet. The tonality centres round a kind of Lydian G flat, with hints of D major, B minor and A flat minor, but, though dance-like, the melodies and rhythms always preserve a vocal flexibility manifested most clearly in the nature of the tonal transitions. An especially lovely instance is this transition into B minor :

and the whole movement is an idyllic marriage of the principles of voice and dance.

The introduction to the finale is founded almost entirely on the opening phrase of drooping semitone, rising sixth and descending tritone ; though quiet, the music is concentrated :

After a while it broadens into a six-eight rhythm, with many of the lyrical lines flowing freely across the bar-lines, and subsides on to a B minor triad in throbbing syncopated triplets on the trombones, around which the strings indulge in quasi-canonic dialogues developing the opening phrases, particularly rising and falling sixths. The music gathers power with a noble entry on the trumpets and trombones, and then is suddenly stilled, a whispered repetition of the opening phrase over a distant timpanum reference to the rhythm of the climax leading directly into the finale, Allegro maestoso.

Although the finale has no 'thematic relation' with the introduction it is felt to be its necessary consummation. It opens polyphonically with a big swaying melody on horns and violins with a counter-subject on trombones and violas, over a descending scale ostinato in the Phrygian mode. Rubbra's fondness for the ostinato is perhaps his only legacy from his teacher Holst, whose music so often owes its somewhat exacerbated nervous force to the tension between the wavering prose-rhythms of his lines and the rigidity of the ostinatos which he employed in order to give them stability. Rubbra's lines, though equally free, are much more lyrical and song-like than Holst's so that the force of his music is less, as it were, frustrated ; but the combination of his 'English sixteenth-century' lyrical sense with a partiality for the dynamic ostinato is obviously relevant to his preoccupation with the texture-shape problem, for you cannot have a more rigid shape than perpetual repetition. It does give his music at times a concentration which, as J. A. Westrup pointed out, reminds one of Purcell, who also occupies a transitional position in the matter of texture and shape[4]. The parallel, however vague, certainly suggests the centrality of Rubbra's place in the English tradition.

In some ways the melody of this finale is one of the most remarkable and distinguished Rubbra has created. It has a bold heroic quality in its enormous sweep and rhythmic vitality and freedom, while at the same time its subtle tonal feeling, shifting between Aeolian, Phrygian and major and minor third, with occasional pungent tritones, seems to imbue its lyricism with an emotion deeply melancholy. It is both heroic and completely contemporary—without any of the limiting nostalgia that, say, Bax's 'heroic' finale tunes are prone to :

(See example top of next page.)

As the melody grows the rhythm and tonality become clearer and bolder (the bouncing dotted rhythm continuing throughout in the counter-subject), and the underlying ostinato acquires first F sharp, then C sharp (the main melody is now more or less in B minor), then G sharp; and finally D sharp, when we have arrived at a lucid E major.

There is then a sudden piano enharmonic transition to E flat minor-like tonalities, the ostinato moving to rising fourths, followed by a further falling to D major, the melodies broadening to a 'meno mosso' section which both increases and, as it were, suspends the excitement by the oscillations of its tonal centre around B, E Flat and E.

4 It is significant that in this (*Listener*) article Mr. Westrup compares Rubbra's Fourth both to the sixteenth-century masters and to Handel—the supreme exponents of texture and shape, respectively. While I see what he means by the reference to Handel, I think the comparison is misleading and that his reference to Purcell makes the same point more accurately. Mr. Westrup's article is an excellent introduction to the general principles of Rubbra's work.

A triplet figure in the accompaniment grows into a quiet E flat major-minor interlude making use of falling fourths. This leads by way of a quasi-canonic duet between flutes and cellos, to a return of the original movement over repeated dominant sevenths of D, in the double-dotted rhythm, while strings evolve flowing triplets in thirds from the accompanying triplets of the flute-cello duo. The seventh G of the bass falls chromatically to E and the ostinato of the opening is re-established with the original subject and counter-subject and a new theme, growing from the rocking triplets of the strings, soaring on top. The tonal clarifying of the melodies and ostinato proceed as earlier in the movement until the establishment of diatonic E major introduces a massive chorale-like theme in canon which, although it has not previously been referred to (if one discounts the fact that the curl downwards of a tone and the return to the tonic are an important ingredient of it) is manifestly the consummation not only of the movement but of the whole work. Music of such direct nobility is to be found nowhere else in immediately contemporary music, except for Vaughan Williams's Fifth Symphony; but its canonic concentration is proof of an integrity and sanity that is more than merely technical. Although the tune is *trionfale* it is certainly not gay; it is experience arrived at through the pride and sinewy sadness of the trumpet melody of the earlier part of the movement, a melody at once actively human in its lyrical buoyancy and lonely and remote in its tonal elusiveness. The final E major trombone triads of the 'chorale' seem to imply a reference back to the syncopated rhythm of the D major end of the first movement—the *con moto's* droop to the flattened seventh has curled back proudly to the tonic. The Symphony is an experience and an affirmation of faith.

If one asks faith in what? one may answer without facetiousness : in itself. While keeping as close to the text of the music as I could, I have tried in these notes to give some idea of what seems to me the approximate equivalent of the music in humanistic or emotional terms, as one must do in any attempt to use words to say anything about music; but obviously such an attempt is bound to be in some degree subjective. I have tried to give a little technical support (*e.g.* the lyrical and vocal nature of the lines, the treatment of the dominant seventh, etc.) to my feeling that the work is 'serene' and 'triumphant', if not easily so; and I think I could give some reasons why I disagree with those critics who seem to feel that it is 'stark' and 'unhappy'. But as Rubbra himself has pointed out in a broadcast talk on the work, though one may say that at this point or that the music has this or the other emotional characteristic, such clumsy translations cannot stand in lieu of the music which can be fully apprehended only in and for itself, *qua* music. The Symphony is not 'about' anything, but is, in the philosophical sense, an 'essence'. This, which is ultimately true of all music though perhaps less obviously so of the representative music of the nineteenth century, is another way of insisting on the essentially 'textural' nature of the work, and brings us back to the point from which these notes started. Rubbra's Fourth is not the 'representation' of a pattern of experience which exists outside itself, but is itself a self-subsistent world with its own laws of germination, growth, bloom and decay. The ultimate mystery of art is perhaps that this world is *also* a quintessence of human experience, but it is not to be understood by crude parallels, nor at all save by accepting it and listening to it on its own terms. Writing about music amounts, or should amount, to an effort to train its readers in the apprehension of the musical organism; it should make them more eager to listen.

III

In concentrating, in this analysis, largely on the significance of Rubbra's treatment of the dominant seventh, particularly in the first movement, I have of necessity omitted much. For one thing, any adequate account of his orchestration would involve almost a bar for bar dissection because with him orchestration cannot be separated from line, nor line from composition. For instance, my account of the reasons why the so-called 'recapitulation' of the first movement produces so different an emotional effect from the opening—is so serenely consummated whereas the opening was quietly expectant—ignored completely the part played in this metamorphosis by the modified orchestration, especially the picking out of the central motives by the trumpet. In general, the tendency to reserve strings, wood-wind and brass to independent functions, noticeable in the earlier symphonies, is here accentuated, but the increased clarity of the texture of composition means, of course, increased clarity in the orchestration too, and there are none of the angry linear-colouristic oppositions that in the first two symphonies gave the climaxes a nervous intensity slightly disproportionate to their proper musical effect. In the Fourth, the extended use of the trumpet in the finale, which with lines of less distinction might easily have been banal, is exquisitely apposite, as is the dominance of wood-wind and violas in the Intermezzo; while the strings-brass altercation at the climax of the *con moto* is orchestrally one of the most remarkable of Rubbra's achievements. Sometimes theory of what should be appropriate to the delineation of the lines somewhat outruns practice; the lovely passage in the first movement for horns and low strings, which looks so rich and poised in score (and sounds so on the piano), in the Albert Hall at least seemed rather gruff and hollow, but the intention was logical enough, and no doubt better acoustic conditions and more adequate rehearsal would reveal it as completely realized. In any case one must be sure, before criticizing Rubbra's orchestration, that one has fully assimilated the musical material of the passage in question. If one looks for 'tone-colour' for its own sake one may well find Rubbra's orchestration 'ungrateful'. Those people who found the orchestration of Nos. 1 and 2 harsh, ruthless and even painful, and that of No. 4 grey and monotonous, did so largely, I believe, because of a tardiness in accepting a musical outlook fresh and, if by no means obscure, certainly the reverse of superficial. Similar charges were made, contemporaneously, against some of the greatest composers in history[5].

5 If one compares Rubbra's work with that of (say) Aaron Copland, whose music always 'sounds' superbly and whose approach, depending on the sharp, lucid articulation of a sound-pattern rather than on melodic generation, is the polar oppo-

The nature of Rubbra's tonal transitions is another subject which I have glanced over and which is worth a paper
to itself. One uses the word transition rather than modulation because Rubbra's shifts of tonal centre are always
lyrical, linearly conceived, and not primarily harmonic
in significance, and because although continually shifting,
his tonal modifications are fluid rather than abrupt. The
manner in which they tend to centre round an initial tone
is significant; the first and last movements' continual oscillations between E, D and E flat have a general significance
with reference to his method as well as the particular ones
I have referred to. The more extreme transitions, such
as the 'modal' A flat leading to the climax of the *con
moto*, are the more powerful for being tentatively
arrived at.

I have also omitted to mention the remarkable melodic
and harmonic affinities between parts of this work (particularly the six-eight sections of the first movement and
of the introduction to the finale, with their rounded semi-
tonal figure and flowing fourths) and the Symphony No. 3
—affinities which argue, of course, not poverty of invention, but the continuity of Rubbra's thought not only
from movement to movement, but from symphony to
symphony. But despite the inadequacy of these notes, I
have thought it worth while to concentrate on his treatment of the dominant seventh because this is the element
which both spiritually and technically is new in No. 4, and
which indicates the direction along which Rubbra's sensibility is likely to advance. This personal use of the seventh,
and the serenity of spirit which it plays its part
in incarnating, a serenity so rare in the music of
to-day and so increasingly valuable, are certainly explored

---

site of Rubbra's, it is true that Rubbra's music seems to lack
'incandescence' and to be narrowly restricted in its range of
movement. But I think this is an inevitable consequence of
Rubbra's attitude to his art at the present stage of his development; and one does not demand 'variety' of an extended fugal
work of Bach.

further in the marvellous opening to No. 5, in which the voice (the mainspring of texture music) may explicitly come into its own, for Rubbra tells me that the symphony will probably be choral, with words by Henry Vaughan.[6] Some such mating of symphony orchestra and choral polyphony was perhaps implicit in Rubbra's texture-shape problem from the start; certainly one awaits the work expectantly.

Historical ifs are always futile and presumptuous because it is men doing and dying with such apparent lack of discrimination that make history and not the other way round; but I think it is relevant in this connection to enquire what would have happened to the history of symphonic writing if Beethoven had composed his Choral Symphony *after* the last Quartets instead of before; or if he had lived to write the symphonic-choral works which at the time of his death he was planning. Rubbra is not a composer who has any kinship with Beethoven. Closer to the English sixteenth century he has always been relatively a texture composer and has anyway, for all the traditional nature of his materials, one of the most personal and consistent manners of any contemporary composer. But without implying any comparison, I have asked this question at the end of these notes as a means of indicating what I believe, when the history of contemporary music is past history, will be found to be the measure of Rubbra's historical, his evolutionary, significance, assuming that Europe's musical traditions survive. If they do not survive, and are painfully replaced by new ones, the general nature of which I once tried to suggest in an essay on Mahler as key-figure, that will not in any way lessen the intrinsic value of Rubbra's music.

Music Review 1943.

(6) Since this was written, the sketch for the opening of No. 5, composed before Rubbra's call-up, has been transformed into the choral and orchestral setting of Vaughan's *The Morning Watch* (1947).

XI

ALAN RAWSTHORNE AND THE BAROQUE

WHEN, DURING THE EIGHTEENTH and nineteenth
centuries, the English musical tradition gradually
declined, fundamentally for social and economic reasons,
one of the symptoms of decay was our failure to absorb
the significant trends of contemporary musical evolution.
It is, for instance, pertinent that although Haydn and
Mozart were frequently played in London in the first half
of the nineteenth century they exerted virtually no
influence on our contemporary composers, who were
unable to assimilate the implications of their sonata idiom.
The great social-dramatic phase of instrumental evolution
we simply by-passed, so that it is hardly surprising that
when Holst and Vaughan Williams came to work
towards the renaissance of our musical culture they
should have returned to the great days—to Tudor polyphony and, behind that, folk-song and hence to a
fundamentally vocal conception of their art. (The unique
case of Elgar, whose magnificently ripe symphonies are
as it were the culmination of a symphonic tradition that
had never happened, we may legitimately regard as a
'sport' in our musical history.)

Most of our best music has been, and I think still is,
vocal in conception. For instance, when Edmund Rubbra
comes to make a consistent attempt to solve the symphonic
problem as it appears to a British composer of our time,
he significantly approaches it from a vocal-polyphonic
standpoint. But there has developed of recent years an
increasing tendency for our composers to try to compensate
for our lack of an instrumental and operatic tradition, to

catch up on two hundred years of musical evolution. The work of Britten in opera and Tippett in oratorio is an attempt to start again where our Restoration composers failed, taking account, of course, of all that has happened in between. And the writing of operatic music entails the linking of vocal technique with instrumental stylizations, just as baroque opera marked an essential transitional stage between the vocal polyphonic outlook and the instrumental sonata architecture.

Now almost alone among contemporary British composers, except perhaps Bliss, Alan Rawsthorne seems to think basically in instrumental terms. His achievement is, however, more closely related to Britten's and Tippett's than such an account would superficially suggest, because the kind of instrumental thinking which he favours is the baroque rather than that of the second half of the eighteenth or the nineteenth centuries. If Britten and Tippett link up with our failure to attain an adequate operatic stylization at the end of the seventeenth century, Rawsthorne links up with our early eighteenth century failure to attain to a classical stability of instrumental architecture.

Purcell was both a local composer and a European; by the eighteenth century any organic connection between the local and the European had for us almost vanished. In this sense Rawsthorne had a more difficult task in achieving a consistent idiom than a composer who could start from the implications of the spoken and sung language. He was bound to use an idiom which had no very obvious connection with the English tradition; indeed he is the only English composer of consequence who has persistently used the kind of idiom loosely referred to as 'central European'. While he has never been an atonalist he has developed an instrumental extension of diatonicism rather along the lines of Hindemith's idiom—or at least of those features of it which relate back to the baroque figuration of Bach. I have already suggested that the re-creation of a baroque stylization is of central importance to the English tradition; what is remarkable is the ease and apparent spontaneity with which Rawsthorne has woven what looks like a foreign idiom into the texture of our native musical attitudes.

For although Rawsthorne's idiom is quite unlike that of any other British composer, it has evolved with complete consistency. He never seems to have had any doubt about the direction in which he wanted to go, and his music is singularly 'of a piece'. The basis of his music is melody. This melody may attain to a long sustained lyricism which, though it is not 'like' Bach, is the product of similar attitudes of mind; a decorative instrumental modification of plastic cantabile line, phrased usually on the analogy of stringed instruments. Of this lyricism the slow and more rhapsodic movements of the Viola Sonata and the two-violin Variations provide admirable instances; still finer is the continuous cantilena of a passage such as this from the chaconne of the Piano Concerto :

Although the peculiar poise of this is attained through the interplay of the melody with harmonic and rhythmic elements to be referred to later, we may note the carefully balanced contours of the line, the placing of the dissonant tensions of the leaps of major sevenths. As in much of Bach's lyrical writing the regularity of the metrical pulse is dissolved in the fluidity and continuity of the melody.

But this plastic lyricism is only one aspect of the melodic nature of Rawsthorne's music; a perhaps more frequent mode is a type of agile contrapuntal writing in which, as in Bach, the rigidity of a persistent motor-rhythm is counteracted by the 'violin-like' nature of the phrasing. Almost all his quick movements are built on this principle; and the contrapuntal writing of the fast movements of the two-violin Variations presents the technique in its simplest and most lucid form.

A further counteraction of the rigidity of metre is provided by the freedom of the tonal transitions; there is rarely a key 'centre', the shifts of tonality being, as in Hindemith, kaleidoscopic. The tonal impression, though ambiguous, does not, however, tend to vagueness. The second of the little piano Bagatelles can begin in C major and end with some unison C sharps with an effect of complete inevitability; and the explicit or implicit insistence on the common triad, through all the tonal vagaries, preserves some kind of harmonic criterion. The opening of the first Bagatelle is characteristic, mingling a wayward subtlety in the tonal transitions with great virility in the resonance of the major triads :

The manner in which, in the Piano Concerto passage
already quoted, the cantilena, soaring over the continually
shifting triads of the accompanying figure, repeatedly produces a major-minor ambiguity in the harmony is pervasive
in Rawsthorne's music, and adds the rather tart, astringent
flavour to his mating of solid diatonic triads with an
extreme tonal instability. He also often employs a decorative chiaroscuro of harmonies, usually thirds or sixths
involving false relations, in regularly floating patterns
which parallel the decorative elements of his lyrical
writing :

Such an effect as this from the chaconne of the Piano
Concerto relies partly on the clarity of the articulation of
the sound pattern ; there is a beautiful passage a little
further on in the movement in which strings and wood-
wind weave pianissimo figurations in sixths (involving persistent major-minor clashes) around the piano's relentless
unfolding of the chaconne rhythm. Throughout one might
say that Rawsthorne's conception of 'free' dissonance is
intimately related to his conception of texture, the articulation of the mosaic of sound ; he uses it to give 'edge'—
a curious tingling quality—to the contour of his lines and
the mould of his formal architecture.

From the formal standpoint, Rawsthorne is unequivocally a baroque composer with his roots in the formal
conceptions of Corelli and Bach. He is never a dramatic
symphonic composer in the sense that Beethoven or even
Mozart is, depending on the development of thematic
motives through contrasts of tonal centre. His notions of
form are rather architectural and decorative and have two
main prototypes in the baroque music of the seventeenth

and early eighteenth centuries—the variation and the concerto grosso, the latter comprising toccata technique (decorative arabesque or passage work), cantilena or aria, fugal elements related to the old fantasia technique, and the formalism of the dance.

Rawsthorne's conception of variation is not the melodic one of Haydn and Mozart but rather that of Bach in the 'Goldberg' Variations and Couperin in the *Folies Françaises*. The ground-bass technique was one of the first (and most primitive) means whereby early baroque composers endeavoured to compose works built on a dance foundation which could none the less attain to considerable dimensions, and its apparently stringent limitations seem to have inspired Purcell, Couperin, and Bach to some of their most intensely passionate, because *intensely* disciplined, music. The chaconne of Rawsthorne's Piano Concerto, though making no pretensions to grandeur, likewise achieves a peculiar emotional power from a latent tension between the passionate contour of the melodic line already referred to, and the relentless pulse of the ground-bass, here repeated, with a cumulative intensity, not at the same level but on ascending degrees of the chromatic scale. The disturbing effect of the music comes from the combination simultaneously of eloquence and tension in the line and harmony with regularity and objectivity in the rhythm and structure. A similar characteristic is observable on, of course, an incomparably more tragic scale in Couperin's great B minor *Passacaille*.

While the chaconne of the piano Concerto is naturally the clearest example of Rawsthorne's connection with baroque technique, the two-violin Variations, the string quartet Variations, and even Rawsthorne's biggest and most important work, the Symphonic Studies, are more freely based on the same notion of the variation form. In all the principle of development is cumulative over an harmonic skeleton that is hardly more than latent; and in all it is this skeleton which gives such tautness to the often very passionate melodic and figurative elements. We may note, too, that even the little piano Bagatelles have a kind of nodal, generative figure common to all of them.

About the nature of Rawsthorne's aria technique no more need be said than was implicit in our remarks about his lyrical sense in general; his aria-like movements manifest always his combination of lyrical fervour with balanced architectural discipline. Nor is much comment necessary on his toccata technique, of which the finest example is perhaps the first movement (capriccio) of the Piano Concerto. Such movements are developed manifestations of his 'decorative' figuration, in which texture and colour combine with the glitter of the fleeting dissonances to create a patterned mosaic of sound—or rather harmonic, textural and colouristic elements are interdependent aspects of the total impression. Sometimes this decorative technique is combined with a dance formalism, as in the tarantella of the same work. The harmonic quality of the figuration again gives an astringent tang to the music's irrepressible gaiety—a rather eldritch Busoni-like atmosphere which prepares one for the unexpectedly moving coda in which, the movement stilled, the music flickers remotely out after some crystalline dissonances on the piano.

Perhaps I can best indicate the nature of Rawsthorne's achievement through what is, perhaps, a more personal impression. Frequently I find in listening to the Piano Concerto or Symphonic Studies, that some recollection of the late work of Vaughan Williams comes into my mind. One would not think that the idiom which I have tried briefly to analyse would have much in common with the most English of composers; that this kind of kinship would seem to be there, however latent, is I think convincing testimony to the manner in which Rawsthorne, without, of course, consciously thinking about it, has absorbed and digested the foreign elements of his idiom into an English sensibility. His music combines lyrical tension and rhythmic energy with great concision and a mordant wit. It has in abundance the virtues which English music at the turn of the century conspicuously lacked ; and it is fundamentally serious and unfacetious. I regret that I have been unable to refer in these notes in more than general terms to the Symphonic Studies, since circumstances have made it impossible for me to have access to a score. But my recollection of this work suggests that there is no composer of his generation potentially capable of making a *more* significant contribution to our musical history, and only three of a comparable stature. The only disquieting feature is that Rawsthorne's output is so exiguous, and that prolonged creative inactivity during the war years can hardly have helped in this direction. It seems to me very important, for himself and for British music, that much Rawsthorne music should be written, and performed, during the next few years.

Tempo, March, 1946.

XII

MASTER OF
THE KING'S MUSIC 1942

FROM THE ANONYMOUS MINSTRELSY of the court of Edward IV, to the direction of the string and wind band of Henry VIII, and thence to the resplendent orchestra, founded on French models, of the court of Charles II, the office of Master of the King's Music (the title was first used, it would seem, of a foreigner, Nicholas Lanier, in 1626) was entirely professional and executive. His function was to assist at courtly entertainments, an executive musician with clearly defined practical duties as a *chef d'orchestre*. As time has gone by and music has become less intimately associated with monarchs, the duties of the Master of the King's Music, like those of the Poet Laureate, have grown broader and less specific; he has become less a courtly than a national institution. But if the function of the Master of the King's Music is now vague, it is not entirely meaningless. Some intimation of the change is perhaps implicit in the case of William Boyce who, succeeding to the office in the middle of the eighteenth century, was not so much a performer as a minor composer and a collector and preserver of the masterpieces of sixteenth and seventeenth-century church music at a time when, of course, anything other than contemporary music was normally regarded in a very patronising spirit. To-day, the Master of the King's Music should act as a focal point of the musical life of our society; he should sum up the trends of creative impulse in the country; he should as a distinguished teacher preserve and strengthen the national musical heritage and influence the nature of musical education from elementary school to academy; and, as a relatively minor part of his activity, he should be able to produce effective occasional music if it should be necessary. I suppose creative ability is not an absolutely essential requirement: but he will certainly do all these things more adequately and more richly if he is himself a creative artist. Perhaps it is significant of the passive rather than active nature of our musical culture in the twentieth century that the late Master of the King's Music, Sir Walford Davies, should have been not a creative artist, but essentially a teacher and expositor. Nowadays we 'appreciate' music so much that we have no time left to make it.

In living memory the one unquestionably valid Master of the King's Music was Sir Edward Elgar, and I think the reason for this was partly because Elgar was a genius, partly because he was probably the last composer unequivocally to endorse and to be endorsed by a social order. Elgar was a great creative artist; but it was just as natural for him to compose *Pomp and Circumstance* and the other occasional musics that so alarm the purists as it was for him to compose the *Introduction and Allegro* or the *Enigma Variations*. One may deplore the enormous gap, in the matter of value, between Elgar's 'serious' and his 'occasional' work; one may think that it witnessed to a certain disintegration, relative at least to Byrd's or Purcell's England, implicit in the society that produced him; but at least that disintegration had not gone so far that one could not recognize the good and the bad as emanating from the same hand. The 'good' things may have embodied the virtues of Edwardian civilization as consummated in its greatest genius, the 'bad' things may have embodied the superficial, tawdry and even repulsive aspects of that civilization; none the less it was the *same* civilization, homogeneous thus far, that we can see that even the bad things might potentially have been virtues, had they not taken the wrong turning. The case of Elgar's bad music is therefore much simpler than that of, say,

Sibelius's, for there is nothing in Sibelius's background to account for the fact that the mind that created the *Fourth Symphony* should also have written *Finlandia* and the drawing-room pieces for piano. Besides, much of Elgar's bad music is so devilishly effective. Even to-day, the Pomp and Circumstances will bring tears to the eyes and lumps to the throat of bare-headed multitudes : if you believe in this kind of thing (and in our half-hearted way we still do or are increasingly supposed to) you may as well indulge with manly gusto instead of a compromising snivel.

To Elgar as Master of the King's Music the obvious successor was, and is, Vaughan Williams—not such a great composer, but an equally great personality, and a more intelligent man, as befits our greater sophistication. Vaughan Williams is so much the most commanding personality in English music over the last thirty years that it is difficult to imagine that the English musical renaissance could have happened without him. Perhaps it would, if more slowly ; but certainly there is no one man to whom English music owes so much, not only for his creative work, but for the importance of his part in the re-establishment of the English Tudor heritage, and of British folk music behind that—branches of his activity from which his creative work can hardly, of course, be separated. Moreover, Vaughan Williams has not only been the mainspring of creative musicians in this country : he has also been indefatigable in his efforts to re-establish a national musical culture that is more than a matter for artists. He has written and arranged quantities of music for schools and colleges, and he has composed stirring music for every kind of national festival that offered itself—none of it bad as Elgar's is bad, none of it perhaps as tritely effective and even inspired. He is still writing 'household' music and unison choral songs of courage and victory and has virtually been Master of the King's Music for the last twenty or more years. Why he has not officially received the title I do not know. Maybe he was not offered it, not having quite the right kind of friends; maybe when it was offered he wouldn't accept. But if the office means anything it is one to be filled by a man with Vaughan Williams's record, and with his capabilities.

In lieu of V.W., I should have thought that William Walton was the obvious choice, especially considering the depressingly well-meaning self-conscious Elgarizing in which Walton indulges in his own occasional music. (At least Elgar meant what he said, though one may not like it very much, whereas Walton is merely pretending or perhaps wishing to feel as Elgar felt in his most pompous and circumstantial mood.) I suppose Walton stood no chance because of the curious notion, nurtured in the nineteenth century, that no one is capable of mastering the King's Music until he has reached the age of sixty; however this may be, I must admit that the appointment to the office of Sir Arnold Bax seemed to me both surprising and perverse.

I do not intend this as a reflection on Bax's talents; merely it seems to me that he has played no part in English musical life, that he has done nothing to mould the English renaissance, and that in his creative work he is neither altogether a contemporary composer nor representatively an English one. All the qualifications that make Vaughan Williams so obvious a candidate, Bax lacks; almost his only qualification is his prodigious facility, and this is a somewhat dubious asset except in so far as it will enable him, if necessity arises, to produce occasional works almost without noticing and therefore without dissipating energies that might be more profitably employed.

I have been listening recently to the records of the Bax album of the English Music Society, and the three works here recorded seem neatly to sum up his virtues and defects. The Nonet, like far too much of Bax's music, is a perfunctory work in which the surface gesture is substituted for true musical substance. Bax, though at his best he is more, is, to begin with, a belated nineteenth-century romantic rhapsodist, and like all such composers he has to work at high pressure for his music to sound convincing. Like Delius, he is at his best when dealing with a solo instrument or voice which rhapsodically soars above, and gives contour and virility to, senuous chromatic harmony and quivering orchestral colour. But his harmony has little of that volatile quality—that unending ebb and flow in the component lines—that makes it almost possible to refer to Delius's technique as 'harmonic polyphony', and in the Nonet and other works in which he is mainly interested in the exploitation of colour and of sonorous device the flow of the chromaticisms is not powerful enough to give the work coherence; it becomes a galli-maufry of ill-collated impressions which, stripped of their colouristic and harmonic decoration and reduced to melodic ideas, seem at best uninteresting and at worst unequivocally tawdry. Of course, the Nonet, being unassuming, is in patches charming and a very beautiful noise; but fundamentally its faults are, I think, the same as those which, in more pretentious works such as the first two piano sonatas, produce so unsympathetic an impression of rhodomontade. Significantly enough, the writing for the instrument itself becomes, in the sonatas, for all its volubility, curiously frustrated and ineffective.

Bax's music is 'fat' music and we all, nowadays, find stringency more congenial : but if the Nonet confirms one's prejudices the other two works in this volume indicate how dangerous it is, with a composer as facile as Bax, to jump to conclusions, for both, if limited, are extremely beautiful, moving and original creations. The Sonata for viola and piano is one of the composer's most concentrated and con-sistent works, and here the experiments in sonorous balance —which are lovely and unusual, particularly the use of the silvery top registers of the piano against the lower range of the viola—are directly the product of the musical material, rather than substitutes for it. The lyrical ideas, plentiful and sustained and of a ripe quality

romantically song-like in its suave conjunct motion and
heroically leaping octaves and fifths, seem themselves to
dictate the tone colour and the placing of the keyboard's
chromaticisms ; indeed the viola is probably the instrument
closest to Bax's vein of mellow, elegiac 'Celtic' lyricism.
The first movement is a rhapsody which slowly merges
out of whispered phrases and then subsides into quivering
silence. The Scherzo, in Bax's 'barbaric' rhythmic manner,
is finely incisive, modal and pentatonic in melodic feeling,
free of any of the padding and empty passage-work into
which this type of movement may easily degenerate ; and
contains a beautiful, celtic-flavoured, folk-song-like trio.
The final lento begins with a widely arching line containing suddenly piercing leaps of seventh and ninth, with
acute dissonant chromaticisms in the piano part, and then
merges into an epilogue, based on material from the first
movement extended and resolved, that attains to a tender
radiance, a kind of purgation, an almost classic sense of
poignant feeling disciplined, which is very rare in music
that so habitually wears its heart on its sleeve. It is, of
course, a music of nostalgia ; but I did not find that it
cloyed on repeated hearings.

The other work, the choral *Ora Mater Filium,* starts
rather like a Peter Warlock chromatic reinterpretation of
mediaeval polyphony, but as soon as it gets into its stride
becomes a completely original choral creation of considerable importance. And its originality does not consist
so much in harmonic resource—or at least only incidentally
—as in the extraordinary efflorescence of the linear rhapsody. The enormous rhapsodic growth of the lines, shooting
and whirling in tremendous spans, becomes at the
climaxes so elaborate as to be almost heterophonic ; and
the balance of the vocal resources, the daring of the
chromatic and diatonic harmonic relations, though
brilliant in themselves, are of those whirling lines genuinely
the product. The premises the music starts from are
mediaeval ; and yet the resultant achievement of the

astoundingly effective and difficult vocal writing is unlike anything else in English musical history and is an achievement which, if it seems to have but little connection with the contemporary world, certainly does not seem to bear any obvious relation to past worlds either. This music lives in a wild sumptuous universe of its own creation, a world of fabulous magic which Bax attains to only once or twice in his whole prolific output—in the Third Symphony and the Symphonic Variations, for instance—but which is, I think, even more than the elegiac nostalgia of the Viola Sonata, what makes his contribution fundamentally a valuable one, if one very much on the margin of English music.

But it is as a symphonist that Bax would wish to be recognized, and to recognize him is difficult because it seems to be next to impossible to hear the works performed, partly owing, no doubt, to their great complexity and to the resources they call for. The case for the prosecution used to say that Bax's symphonies sound like the same symphony seven times over; or, with Mr. Constant Lambert, that they are not symphonies at all but extended symphonic poems. The first of these charges, considering the scanty opportunities for hearing the music, is perhaps merely flippant; and as for the second, one must remember that it is not legitimate to introduce an act of uniformity against symphonists. Though one may feel (ignorantly) dubious of following Edwin Evans and Robin Hull, among others, as far in the contrary direction as to claim that Bax's symphonies, if performed and studied, would be recognized as an achievement comparable in importance and scope with those of Sibelius, one is bound to admit that these works do manifest tremendous creative energy. Their carefully complex formal processes—their 'embryonic' introductions, polyphonic-cum-chromatic-harmonic evolution, and apotheotic epilogues consummating the emotional temper of the whole three-movement work—are, if tensely handled, as musically logical as the more specifically elliptical methods of Sibelius, and show a consistent attempt to achieve order both emotional and musical out of the immense exuberance of the composer's rhapsodic zest : any other meaning there may be in the words 'symphonic form' is after all a matter of academic interest only. Of Bax's symphonies, I have never heard No. 5 (which many people consider the finest) or No. 6 ; and my acquaintance with Nos. 1, 2 and 7 is too superficial to give adequate backing to my feeling that they are excessively violent and sultry in their subjective emotionalism. But No. 4 is a very beautiful, ripely romantic composition in which the exquisite orchestration is inseparable from the flow of the lines, culminating in the triumphantly vibrant epilogue ; and No. 3 still more, is a big work, heroic in its weird antediluvian way, with the sinister orchestral colouring again created by the nature of the lyrical material, with the slow mysterious glimmer of its opening and the expansive exotic pageantry and ultimate serenity of the choral-like close. (There is a distant hint of this in Bax's personal use of 'English' parallel fifths in the first movement of the Viola Sonata.) But when it is genuine (it may easily become a mere formula) Bax's pageantry could hardly be said to be of an 'occasional' order : and one cannot help thinking it odd that the creator of this dark universe of primeval gods and satyrs should have become the honoured guardian of British musical respectability. Perhaps there is some virtue merely in the extent of the output ; being so vast, the few things in it that really matter may easily pass unnoticed, along with their 'unacceptable' implications.

XIII

CONSERVATISM AND TRADITION

POST OBITUM
DONALD FRANCIS TOVEY
HAMILTON HARTY
FRANK BRIDGE

THERE CAN BE NO reasonable doubt that the influence
of the late Donald Francis Tovey on our musical life was
incommensurably greater than one would gather from his
published works, creative or critical. As a pianist and con-
ductor he displayed—what so few professional virtuosi
possess—great historical knowledge and the understanding
of a thorough musician, combined with sensitiveness and
sympathy, yet one could hardly claim that he was among
the supreme creative performers of history. As a composer
his work is so steeped in his learning—his knowledge of
other men's music, particularly Haydn's and Beethoven's
—that it sounds like mere pastiche or student's exercise
until one has learned to respond to the authentic Tovey
flavour ; and even then its models are such unexpected
ones for a contemporary composer that one cannot help
responding to it rather as one would to a horticultural
sport, so that it is difficult not to over or under-estimate
it according to one's personal proclivities. Even his written
works are few and almost casual, occasioned more by
pressure of circumstances (programme notes or lectures)
than by any desire to commit his reflections to the relative
durability of print. Yet he must have been one of the
greatest teachers—of any art—in our time ; and he pre-
ferred talking to writing. The two posthumous volumes[1]

1 *A Musician Talks*, by Donald Francis Tovey. (Oxford Press,
in two volumes, Vol. 1 *The Integrity of Music*, Vol. 2, *Musical
Textures*

are valuable mostly for their very informality; because
they convey the accent of Tovey's talk and thereby the
essence of his musical creed; because they indicate his
notions as to what musical education ought to be, notions
which informed equally his most conversational epigram
about music and the scholarship of the Bach editions and
the *Companion to the Art of Fugue.*

I do not think it is true to suggest that Tovey made any
profoundly original or revolutionary statements about the
art which he practised so assiduously. The beliefs he held
by should be, but are not, common-places of musical
æsthetics; his importance lies in his expressing them with
a precision that convinces and an authority that awes. He
had an unparalleled knowledge of European music, particularly of the classical epoch, and he used his knowledge never as dead matter to clutter the intelligence
but as material for the intelligence to work upon.
To read these books is to realize the source of his
greatness as a teacher; to be aware of the embracing
coherence of his point of view, of how he taught his pupils
that most difficult task, to think consistently in musical
terms. The basis of his tenets is that technique and
æsthetics are inseparable, so that the detail and elaboration
of his technical investigations in the *Essays in Musical
Analysis* becomes of importance not merely to the professional but to all those concerned about music as a manifestation of the human spirit. It is, I think, a weakness
of the essays that one might not, from internal evidence,
always be aware of this : these last books make it clear
that if one had been taught by him one could have no
doubts.

A somewhat lengthy list of quotations will demonstrate
this more clearly than any review of these volumes'
contents :

    The teachers of strict counterpoint merely added
    the stiffness of modern tonality to the restrictions of
    pure sixteenth-century polyphony, entirely failing to see

that those restrictions and the freedom and variety of
the Church modes were intimately related . . . Nothing
that concerns the composer as a means to an end can
be separated from that end. Counterpoint is the art
by which a combination of good melodic lines produces
complete harmony without the need of any inferior
accessory matter. It is ridiculous to say that such art
is only a means and not an end in itself. If the counterpoint, with or without accessory matter, is not beautiful,
why complain that it is too ingenius? It is not ingenious
at all . . . It so happened that during the career of
Palestrina . . . the purists were the persons of far-sighted
intellect and, roughly speaking, we may say that it
was the inaccurate artists who were dull. At no later
period in musical history has the academic theory been
so completely in harmony with the finest musical
inspiration of contemporary composers.

The harmony of the dramatic sonata style of Haydn,
Mozart and Beethoven is in detail simpler than that of
Bach, because you cannot build large-scale relations of
key on a basis of elaborate harmonic detail, any more
than you can construct a dramatically exciting play out
of epigrams. Beethoven's harmony may become as
abstruse as the profoundest of Bach's figured chorales
if his task allows him to devote a short section of a
work to matters of a local harmonic interest, as in the
Variations on a waltz of Diabelli . . . You cannot con-
ceive that any movement of the B minor Mass should
need some merely architectural chords to complete it;
but when musicians regard the last forty-odd bars of
Beethoven's C minor Symphony as a meaningless noise
they are as far from truth as the most naïve listener to
whom a fugue is a tuneless chaos. These forty bars are
meaningless without the rest of the symphony, but the
symphony ends as truly within its own length as the
'Et in terra pax' of the B minor Mass.

The difference between Bach and Handel consists

largely in the fact that Bach is so continually adding
pioneer work to his routine that the pioneer work itself
rapidly forms into habits, whereas Handel exerts himself only when the Bible or other special circumstances
arouse him . . . If the burden of knowledge is too great
for the artist, his remedy is not to have less knowledge
but to have more habit and experience in the handling
of it . . . Great inspiration is indistinguishable from
first-rate athletic form, whether mental or physical.

If we can see no more in Beethoven's orchestration
than was seen by Rimsky-Korsakov, to whom it was
nearly as obsolete as a tricycle with solid tyres is to the
owner of a Rolls Royce, then we shall certainly not
appreciate, much less achieve, the splendours of
Rimsky-Korsakov's brilliant and meticulously pure
orchestration; and though we may easily emulate the
perky provinciality and pedantry of his mind, we shall
suffer in our own estimation from the hopeless dis-
advantage of being British, whether Northern or
Southern, instead of having the privilege of being
Russian, and therefore romantic and exotic.

Knowledge of Bach's orchestration is obtained
through historic research, but it becomes a set of purely
æsthetic principles inherent in the music.

No mature work of art is wonderful 'for the time at
which it was written'. It is simply wonderful at all
times. A naïve belief is now prevalent that all great
artists have been in advance of their time. The effect
of this doctrine is to make the average artist of the
present day ready to believe that it is his duty to be
unintelligible to his contemporaries. This is not difficult.
All he need do is to be unintelligible to himself . . . It
is more than a living composer's reputation is worth to
be accused of anything more than a private new
æsthetic of his own, but in the time of Beethoven
correctness was the chief criterion in all the arts : and
a very much better and more stimulating criterion it is

than our sterilizing criterion of originality.

If one reads the above quotations carefully one can see implicit in them the centrality of Tovey's position with reference to all the most important subjects he discusses—his notion of the integrity or purity of musical forms ('Wagner is one of the supreme masters of musical forms but the integrity of his art makes this form arise out of the conditions of his drama'), his distinction between musical textures (the polyphonic principle) and musical shapes (the dramatic and architectural sonata), his notion of tonality, of fugue, of musical movement ('The weakness of Bruckner is in his uncritical and helpless retention of the externals of sonata form, for which the pace of his action is hopelessly too slow. Two things are essential to the sense of cosmic movement : firstly it must not be reduced to lower orders of movement by the only possible kind of event that can normally give us a sense of movement at all ; and secondly it must become distinguishable from complete stagnation by the presence of smaller forms of movement, so that we may have a standard of comparison'), and even his discussion of such apparently narrowly technical procedures as recapitulation, the trill in eighteenth-century music, or the setting of words. These things, together with the brilliant account of concerto form in the *Essays in Musical Analysis,* constitute Tovey's enduring contribution to musical æsthetics; and they provide examples, surely, of some (though not all) of the ways in which intelligence should function in *anyone* professing to call himself a musician.

It is important to insist on the centrality of Tovey's position because he has been subjected to an extravagance of hero-worship which has on the one hand represented him as endowed with a superhuman insight into musical problems before which ordinary mortals can only bow their heads in silent homage, and which has on the other hand tended covertly to apologize for the stiffness of his technical reasoning by means of the 'wise and witty' belleslettristic approach. Apart from a donnish strain which occasionally leans towards facetious dedications and elaborate jokes in indices, Tovey has done nothing to deserve either fate : he was an intensely practical musician who devoted his life to an endeavour to teach other would-be practical musicians what the fundamentals of their practicality ought to be. He was not a seer and possibly not a genius ; he was a musician who was not afraid to think and to persuade others to think with him. As such, his kind is so rare that his name will, one hopes, be long venerated.

As Tovey's name will always be associated with Edinburgh, so the name of Sir Hamilton Harty, who died on February 19th, will always be associated with Manchester. He was among the most distinguished of British conductors, not only for the virility and sensitiveness of his performance, but for the enterprise of his programme-making. His performances of the large-scale works of Berlioz, particularly the *Requiem,* will count for me among the supreme musical experiences of a life-time ; since Harty's virtual retirement through ill-health they have never been performed at all. It is odd that one so alert to Berlioz's extremely subtle melodic genius should, in his own compositions, follow the turgid nineteenth-century tradition which is the polar opposite to Berlioz's aristocratic finesse ; his performances of Berlioz were in my opinion more truly creative, of greater significance for the present day, than any of his original compositions which expressed at second hand the feeling, as well as the idiom, of a generation that is lost to us.

And yet I think it was this very generation that gave Harty the moral backbone to use his intelligence and sensitiveness to such effect in less obviously creative fields, so that while having himself neither ability nor desire to feel differently from the generality of his more intelligent contemporaries, he had the power to respond magnificently to other and profounder personalities whose ways of experiencing were indeed unique and irreplaceable. His generation enabled him to make the most of his potentialities whereas nowadays many men, probably equally endowed with talent and intelligence, fail to achieve anything and dissipate their energies for want of any moral backbone. In this sense Tovey and Harty were of the same build : there was an element of greatness in their personalities—a courage, sanity and power—that many who are more creative than Tovey and cleverer than Harty may often be without. Such personalities were never plentiful ; to-day they are rare indeed.

Frank Bridge, the third figure in English musical life who has died this year, was in this respect a representative, I think, of the later generation ; an artist endowed with talent and facility and yet without the moral backbone to bring his gifts to fruition. It is remarkable that though his activities were confined almost entirely to composition and only incidentally to teaching, whereas Tovey and Harty were composers only incidentally, his personality seems much more shadowy than that of either of the two older men. Whereas they had the courage of their convictions in general musicianship, and in their compositions were unpretentiously content with the idiom they were born to, Bridge squandered very great gifts of musicianship through failing to decide what kind of stature he aimed at and what sort of idiom was his by inheritance ; so that if Harty's music belongs to a generation that is lost to *us,* Bridge's music produces in us an uneasy feeling that he was lost to himself. Tovey and Harty, although conservatives in composition, had an intelligence and self-knowledge that forestalled pretension and ambiguity : but Bridge was even conservatively unconservative, writing music in whatever mode happened to be fashionable at the moment—now nineteenth-century academic with folky flavour, now Debussy-cum-Scriabin chromatics, finally even atonalism, just to show, apparently, that he too could do it. Through all the twists of the weather-vane the only stable element is something that amounts to little more than synthetic John Ireland, the one English composer to exert any pervasive influence on Bridge and one whose mannerisms are dangerously easy to acquire. But the 'little more', if it exists, is the point, and I do not mean that Bridge's music is necessarily feebler than Tovey's or Harty's; it may be a good deal more interesting. His conservatism argues, of course, a not very powerful personality; but it is a very delicate task to tell, with a composer who adheres so closely to the veneer of other composer's manners, just how far the manner is used and how far it is a substitute for an original impulse—to tell, for instance, whether there is only a Scriabinesque paraphanalia of tragedy in the Piano Trio—all the superimposed appogiaturas and garish stage-trappings—but none of the tragic substance.

Often I think there is a very real talent in the melodic ideas; but beautiful and striking phrases are not enough to make a composition[2]. Bridge's ideas are too frequently seeds which fail to germinate; they do not grow but some gimcrack floral decoration (copied from last year's fashions) is tied to them with an art that becomes artifice, until the original impulse, which was genuine, becomes submerged beneath a façade of other men's gestures. The explanation is, I think, a deficiency of character—of what I earlier called moral backbone; and too much of Bridge's music demonstrates how those two apparent opposites, the academic and the fashionable, are but two aspects of the same disease of psittacosis. 'Nothing is easier', as Tovey said, 'than to classify musical art-forms and set up their criteria as if they were ideals that existed before the music was made for them'; all Bridge's imitative facility has

2 *cf.* Tovey: 'The teaching of composition and the understanding of music would be greatly advanced if a law were made forbidding the assertion that Beethoven's C minor Symphony is founded on a figure of four notes. Melodies are not built up out of figures. They are large musical objects which are divisible into figures.'

nothing to do with his being or not being an artist.

I believe it is significant that Bridge's best work should have been done in the medium which offers least opportunity for more or less extramusical 'effects'—namely, the string quartet. The Second is a fine vigorous work in Bridge's least chromatic, most traditional (as distinct from academic) vein, while the Fourth, superficially influenced by the Schönbergians, uses the angular leaps and nervous dissonances of that idiom to aggravate an impulse that remains Bridge's own and essentially lyrical. With an habitual technical adroitness the idiom is more freely independent, and more mature, than that of any of Bridge's works of a comparable seriousness. Perhaps, when he died, Bridge was on the point of discovering a language that would have been adequate to, and would thereby to some extent have relieved, the limiting instability of his temperament : an idiom developing in a logical if highly-strung manner that lyrical feeling which was in earlier works fragmentary, but none the less the essence, beneath the eclecticism, of his sensibility and his character as an 'English' rather than an academic and/or fashionable composer. It is no accident that Bridge—an artist representative of the twentieth century in so far as he indicates how conservatism and fashion are secret allies in league against Tradition—should finally have come to terms with a technique which, whatever its potentialities or restrictions, can, apart from mere insular prejudice, with justice be dubbed 'un-English'.

Scrutiny 1942.

XIV

TOWARDS A MUSICAL ACADEMY

I

NOW THAT THE FUNCTION of education needs increasingly precise definition—now that we more than ever need to understand clearly what we expect from education and what we might do to ensure the fulfilment of these expectations—it seems pertinent to offer a few comments on the meaning of the phrase 'musical education', with specific reference to the place such education ought to occupy in a civilized society.

There is to-day fairly uniform agreement that musical education is not all it might be : but this healthy dissatisfaction has proved unavailing partly because those who uphold the present system have forestalled complaints by pointing out that things are not as bad as they used (ten, twenty, thirty years ago?) to be, as though this were adequate ground for complacency; and partly because those who condemn the present system are prone to indulge in the sentimental reflection that musical education as it was (to take the stock example) to the Elizabethans— musical education as a participating activity, part and parcel of everyday life—is dead and done for anyway. This notion is sentimental because it ignores the fact that, whether or not our civilization is inferior to, it is fundamentally distinct from, that of the Elizabethans, that it has its own problems which are not incapable of solution. If it is true that our approach to musical education must necessarily be more self-conscious, then for that very reason it becomes not less, but more urgent and important that we should attempt some such approach. The attitude of superiority to academic institutions can anyway only do harm to however well-intentioned a cause, because it gives those within the pale a legitimate right to insinuate that the outsider who sneers is either an ignorant amateur, or a crank, or both. A little good-will on both sides is essential if the closed barriers which at present shut off the 'academic' musician from contact with the rest of the civilized world are either to be broken down or voluntarily relinquished.

That it is important that the barriers should be removed can hardly be disputed, for the main difficulty in deciding what one means by musical education lies in that quality of abstraction in the nature of the art which tends to encourage a divorce between music and the other great branches of knowledge (or thought or feeling). Probably this difficulty could be effectively counteracted only during the early stages of education, in which case some conception of the rudiments of musical grammar and of musical history should be taught in schools not as a specialized activity but as one of the great departments of human knowledge, as central as literature or science or mathematics. The idea of music as an art to which only the technically initiated have access should be rigorously guarded against, and I know of no way of ensuring this except to stress continually the relation between the musical manifestations of the human spirit and the verbal, plastic, pictorial, mathematical and particularly historical ones[1]. Certainly under the present system the potentially musical child may often languish for lack of impetus to his imagination, whereas a relatively unmusical child will be pushed through a course which it finds acutely boring merely because it has betrayed a certain aptitude for— or manual dexterity on—a particular instrument, usually the piano. Such instrumental prowess would seem to bear

1 I have written in detail on musical education in Schools (incorporating some practical suggestions) in the chapter on Music from *Ends and Means in Education,* edited by Denys Thompson & George Reeves, (Muller).

sometimes an almost fortuitous, and always a very complex, ratio to essential 'musicality'; in any case one cannot work out that ratio merely by dumping a pupil down at a key-board.

This is a difficulty that extends to a more advanced stage of musical education than that tentatively offered by the day-school, for the main function of musical academies as at present constituted is undoubtedly the manufacture of performers. They have other functions; but by far the majority of the students attend academies in order to gain official recognition of their efficiency on a particular instrument. No one would want to suggest that a desire to perform is to be deplored : but probably about one-twentieth of these students—at a liberal estimate—have talent sufficient to justify a professional career. The rest would be better employed in educating themselves to form a responsible and discriminating audience for the talented. Theoretically, the economic objection might be urged that it is no use talking airily about discriminating audiences when the aim of most of these young men and women is eventually to eke what precarious livelihood they can from their professional studies. But this objection is no more than theoretical because only a very small percentage of the students make much use of their technical dexterity in their subsequent careers as teachers, accompanists, church, or even cinema-organists : all they require from their studentship is the 'certificate', and this might as well be awarded for a humane education as otherwise. Neither the ability to play an instrument, nor a knowledge of the grammar of music is, by itself, a contribution towards musical education : the simplest, and yet apparently the most difficult, lesson for a musician to learn is that one cannot be 'musically' educated without being emotionally educated as well. Indeed it is difficult to understand how, without some general, humane, musical education it is possible to train a satisfactory interpreter at all. At this point, the circle completed, we are in a position to ask

what the basis of this general musical education might be.
In a phrase I would summarize it as the inculcation of the
Historical Perspective.

II

I think it may be because music is a relatively abstract
art—its medium remote from the material of every-day
life—that our judgments about it are prone to be more
humanly fallible than they are, perhaps, with any other
art. We imagine ourselves as standing at this particular
minute point in time, looking back almost with com-
placence at the ever-rolling stream, able to assess from our
lofty eminence the size and contour of each particular
wave or ripple. We forget how we fail in consistency—
how to-day's dæmonic Mozart was the child-like cherub
of yesterday. We lack humility; brazenly proclaiming the
subjectivity of our responses we assert its almightiness,
make no effort to temper it with knowledge and understanding of the kind of significance men of ages and creeds
different from our own may have seen in their art.
Egoistically we fall, therefore, into three connected kinds
of error, the first of which may be described as errors
arising from insensitive response to emotional climates;
the second, as errors related to problems of social necessity;
and the third, as purely technical errors consequent upon
the two previous failings.

Of these errors the first, that relating to emotional
climates, is by far the most serious : I will give one main
example of it—the reputation, in this country, of Jean-
Baptiste Lully. Amateurs and academic musicians alike all
know—they can read it in any of the history books—that
although Lully is a composer of 'some historical importance' with reference to the Beginnings of Opera and the
Development of the Orchestra, his music is of antiquarian
interest only, being artificial, superficial, frigid and
altogether devoid of æsthetic import, as indeed one can
only expect from the product of a decadent state of

society. No one, least of all academy students, is ever given an opportunity to put these generalizations to the test since the artificiality, superficiality and frigidity of Lully's music are the reasons offered for never performing it. Instead, Lully is off-handedly compared to his great contemporary, Purcell, whose human, passionate and dramatic music (itself almost completely unknown less than twenty years ago) is presumably supposed to sum up the entire achievement of the seventeenth century, and is left to bury his head in the sands of oblivion as best he may.

Even without an intimate knowledge of Lully one cannot help feeling uneasy about these glib assumptions, cannot help suspecting that it may be idiotic to look to Lully for the same kind of satisfaction that one finds in Purcell, cannot help remembering that if he lived in a decadent and superficial society, that society was great enough to produce Racine. When one considers the treatment that Racine himself used to be subjected to at the hands of English critics—considers how all the opprobrious adjectives now heaped on the composer were one time the property of the writer—one is bound to tread more cautiously still. Bonnet, in his *History de la Musique* published in 1715, said of Lully 'Did he wish to depict Love, what heart is not melted? And what melody, what naturalness! Did he wish to express Grief, do not the rocks groan with him?' Would hearts have melted and rocks have groaned for a maker of courtly trifles? May it not be that we find Lully's music dull because we listen to it arrogantly, without regard to its conventions and its own emotional climate, if indeed we listen to it at all?

I have dealt at some length with the case of Lully not for its inherent importance but because it is representative. I might have chosen countless other examples. For instance, if the church music of Couperin le Grand—music as profound as anything written in the eighteenth century, not excepting Bach—were even as well known as his clave-

cin pieces which are always dismissed as 'charming' but
'artificial' drawing-room confections, perhaps we might
begin to understand why Couperin himself certainly did
not regard his little pieces as being deficient in seriousness
or emotional intensity merely because their duration
in time was brief and their sonority not excessive. Even
Bach himself, as Schweitzer has shown, might be better
performed if he were better understood; and the further
one goes back in musical history the greater the possibilities
of misapprehension must necessarily be. The poignantly
dramatic Monteverdi or the intense Vittoria offer a more
immediate satisfaction to our ears than the relatively
impersonal Palestrina, but that does not mean that they
are more 'profound'. Nor does it mean that they are more
profound than (say) Guillaume de Machaut. Indeed the
ignorance of and indifference to all pre-sixteenth-century
music displayed in academic institutions is perhaps the
most damaging of all evils consequent upon a deficiency
of historical perspective. Can one seriously maintain that
for several centuries European composers—including men
of the most phenomenal versatility of intellect such as
Machaut and Jacopo da Bologna—tottered helplessly
around on the hollow crutches of their fourths and fifths
because they failed to 'discover' the diatonic third? Isn't
it more reasonable to conclude that they used fourths and
fifths because they liked them? No one thinks of referring
to the 'progress' of the English language from Chaucer
to Shakespeare; it is accepted that they incarnate distinct
civilizations and people making any pretentions to literary
cultivation are willing to make the small effort necessary
to overcome the slight unfamiliarity of Chaucer's language.
Similarly, the conventions of thirteenth and fourteenth
century polyphony may be very different from those of
nineteenth century homophony, but it is the smuggest
obtuseness to claim that the latter are more mature. If
one *listened* to Perotin or Jacopo or Perusio—as one can
do a little with the help of the gramophone—one might

N

begin to realize that such a contention is no less absurd
than that of the history book which claimed to trace the
evolution of European music from the 'infancy' of
Monteverdi to the 'maturity' of Richard Strauss !

Inevitably, therefore, the second class of errors—those
connected with social necessity—is bound up with the
first, since almost all errors of emotional climate arise from
a misguided attempt to listen to music *in vacuo,* or in an
environment inappropriate to it. One cannot hope to
respond 'appropriately' to a musical composition if one is
oblivious of the kind of social significance the composer
intended it to have. One cannot sensitively listen to almost
all so-called primitive musics and the better part of European music up to the sixteenth century if one does not
realize that the connection between music and society,
even between music and behaviour, was here an extraordinarily direct and immediate one, designed as ritual
to induce a certain physiological state in the listener's nervous system. (This is to some extent true even of Palestrina,
which is why he, rather than Vittoria or Lasso, is, in the
hypnotism of his mellifluous linear writing, the
supreme musical expression of the Catholic ritual.) For
Bach music was still 'an harmonious euphony to the glory
of God' and if we fail to realize this our notions of him
will be partial and distorted : but he is also a professional
craftsman making music for a secular and social need, so
that he inaugurates the Professional period which cul-
minates in Haydn and Mozart. Nor can one understand
the music of the nineteenth century aright if one does not
realize why the 'professional' relation between music and
society gave way to the idea of the composer as tragic hero
and why in the twentieth century there have been a number of attempts to provide artificially a relationship that
should be organic—attempts of which the most innocent
is Gebrauchmusik and the most insidious (as well as the
most futile) the allying of music with propaganda.

The technical errors dependent on these first two classes

of error concerning emotional climate and social necessity are too numerous to describe here in any detail; the most I can do is to indicate their range. They include misapprehensions about the phrasing of Bach, particularly his basses; misapprehensions about the nature of eighteenth-century ornamentation which is attributed to a desire to compensate for the inferior mechanism of the 'old instruments', notwithstanding the fact that it appears equally in vocal music and that Couperin himself said 'that it is not a matter of choice to introduce such ornaments as one wishes. I declare that my compositions should be executed as I have marked them and that they will never produce a certain impression on persons of real taste so long as everything I have indicated is not observed to the letter'[2]; misconceptions about the balance of wood-wind and strings, and the importance of the harpsichord, in the eighteenth-century orchestra; failure to appreciate the distinction in kind between viol and violin, harpsichord and piano, baroque organ and modern; and all manner of fallacies of tempo and interpretation arising from a romantic upbringing.

I hope I have established that an Historical Perspective is an indispensable basis for a true musical culture. But what kind of practical training, it will be asked, is likely to conduce to such an attitude? Assuming that a student proceeds to his musical academy with a working knowledge of the grammar of music and that he is at least willing to acquire immediately that ability at score-reading without which he can have first-hand experience of only a microscopic proportion of the music of European history, I believe that such an outlook would emerge naturally from his technical studies providing that these studies were given intelligent direction. In the next section I will attempt to indicate what this direction might be.

2 François Couperin: *L'Art de toucher le clavecin.*

III

In trying to gain, from first-hand experience, a coherent idea of the unfolding tradition of European music one has continually to bear in mind the interaction of four allied aspects of it. These are (i) the composer's creative faculty; (ii) the society of which he is a unit; (iii) the resources available to him—which will be conditioned by (ii); and (iv) the idioms he uses—which will be conditioned by all three previous points in varying degrees, according to the vitality of his personality and the relatively traditional or anarchic nature of the society he lives in. Of course, it is impossible to study all these aspects simultaneously; but we shall understand none of them thoroughly if we are not at least aware of the influence upon it of the others. For instance, one could not study the great monophonic period of European music from plainsong and troubadours to Ars Antiqua without enquiring into the question of why the human voice was the pre-eminent medium when the relation between music and society was prevailingly ritualistic. In considering the nature of the idiom and its relation to the 'material resources' of the voice one would further seek—by way of a number of quasi-digressions into folk-song and possibly non-European musics—to relate the origins of melodic speech to the fundamentals of the human voice and the harmonic series, would examine the nature of melodic subtlety and the expressive advantages, as well as (or rather than) the limitations of music conceived in terms of a single line. Only by studying the sixteenth century idiom in relation to the impetus behind it—the Church and an extremely homogeneous domestic milieu—can one appreciate the full significance of its idiom's derivation from the implications of the voice, its convention of sing-ableness, its melodic rather than metrical notion of rhythm, its polyphonic conception of discord as movement before the concord's repose, the immense importance of the poly-phonic technique as a factor governing composition. With composers such as Purcell or Bach it would be impossible to separate various modifications in the resources available to them—for instance, the increasing use of relatively mechanical instruments—from the nature of the environment they lived in, and it would be impossible to sense the feel of their idioms without regard to the impact their unique creative personalities made on their communities and on their material and vice versa. Study of the fugue with reference to Bach would also elucidate the connection between polyphony and counterpoint—counterpoint as a means of systematizing polyphonic writing—and would indicate how this systematization should be a technical manifestation of the objective, 'classical' organization of experience, and in what ways this is attributable to the composer's genius on the one hand, or to the homogeneous social conditions he flourished in on the other. Obviously an examination of the problem of symphonic form and of the implications of diatonicism could start from the antithesis between an instrumental and vocal technique in an aristocratic society; nor would a study of chromaticism and romanticism (Gesualdo, Liszt, Wagner, Delius, Berg) avail much if it did not indicate the connection between the homophonic conventions, the decay of stable tonalities, and the notion of 'self-expression' and of 'autobiographical' drama. 'Musical' history, moreover, cannot properly be separated from the history of the dance and the stage and to a lesser degree poetry. All these subjects offer more or less complex problems : but I hope I have, even if with rather ironic compression[3], indicated the centrality of the studies which I have in mind.

By 'studying' musical compositions I mean examining, feeling, listening to, performing the scores until one knows them in one's blood and bones : that is the only stable basis for a musical education. In order to examine and

3 The attitude to musical history briefly summarized above is described in detail—with specific reference to England—in my book *Music and Society*.

perform sensitively a certain amount of historical or socio-
logical knowledge is essential, but there should be nothing
irksome about that, if it is directed to the fuller flowering
of the music as such. The student might well work exercises
in the manner of different composers or schools of composers, so long as he realizes that such exercises are nothing
to do with composition but merely help him to understand
the functioning of these idioms more clearly and to
respond more delicately, therefore, to their emotional
climate. In the long run there can, anyway, be no division
between technical training and historical studies—the
training of taste and discrimination—since technique is
merely the outward symbol of an inner grace (or disgrace).
To take a very simple instance, a technical training which
did not enable one to indicate in technical terms why
Chabrier is a composer of comic genius whereas Massenet
is for the most part a hack inculcating the same kind of
response as the Hollywooden hack of to-day whose idiom
to some extent derives from him, would be next to useless; and any knowledge of the workings of music one
could acquire without even realizing that this distinction
existed, would have no more bearing on musical studies
than facility at the unravelling of cross-word puzzles has
bearing on literature. Similarly it is a truism of academic
criticism that Berlioz could not write fugues, presumably
because of defective technique, whereas the only question
worth asking is not: Are Berlioz's fugues 'really' fugues,
but do they, in actual performance, come off? Fugue is
not *a* form but, as Tovey used to say, a texture, a way of
writing, a consequence of the polyphonic outlook. Nor
are there any absolutes of form: the only means of testing
the authenticity of musical forms—including one's own—
is to listen to them. And to learn to listen to music is in
truth the most difficult discipline of all. To the attaining of
it, technical exercises and historical studies are merely a
means; once attained, it leads by implication to the making
of value-judgments about the music which is experienced.

This is why a course on contemporary music, combined with exercises in criticism, should be indispensable to any musical academy. Those who are unable to listen intelligently to and to discriminate between the works of their contemporaries are unlikely to achieve much vital experience of the music of any period ; first-hand response to the unfamiliar should be regarded not as a *jeu d'esprit* but as a fundamental aspect of education.

An obvious criticism of all I have written above is that a musical education of the type here tentatively suggested would be the labour of a life-time. My answer to this is, of course it would. Education is not static : we should, all of us, feel proud if, by the day we die, we have begun to acquire anything of an education at all. No one would suggest that a student who goes to a university to study literature for three years has, when that time has elapsed, completed his education ; he has just about begun it, and this would be true of a musical education, too, even though you would never gather, from the way music is taught at present, that this art also is one of the highest manifestations of the human spirit. All one could hope to do in a few years' training would be to help the student to *listen*, and to direct his attention to those problems most worth considering. Detailed study of the whole of the music of the European tradition would be as unnecessary as it is impossible. How many of the fundamental issues would not be raised by thorough study of (say) Machaut, of English music in the sixteenth and seventeenth centuries (with particular reference to the shift in the social background), of Bach, and of a representative list of composers including Monteverdi, Haydn, Beethoven, Liszt, Berlioz, Rossini and Stravinsky? In any case, by comparing and relating technical traits one would learn to appreciate the human motives that underlie them ; one would acquire a technical training with true direction, not in a vacuum but as applied to the living tissues of musical thought, in all their delicacy, their unceasing fluctuations. This training would become the richer as one's experience of music increased ; and increase it would, for one would now be listening with an enjoyment the deeper for being critical, and the more critical for being used on understanding and love. Only if the stress falls on fundamentals can the mind be trained and the sensibility given that poise and direction —that faculty of organizing one's responses, of knowing where one stands and what one is about—without which education is little more than a futile, if decorative, encumbrance.

IV

Some such course as that suggested above—and I am aware that the framing of the syllabuses would be a delicate matter—should, in my opinion, be the basis of a humane musical education. It would be a training in the essentials of musical tradition and of musical æsthetic, a training in listening which would enable one to respond as fully as possible to the complexities of musical thought, to the organic, as opposed to the paper, evolution of linear contour and harmonic stress. (Responding to music merely as a matter of academic technical procedures is, after all, as remote from the actualities of musical experience as responding to it merely for its power of evoking visual images, or of giving impulse to private nostalgias or day-dreams.) This course, directing their minds towards the source of a stable musical cultivation, would be obligatory on all students ; but it would not, of course, preclude specialized studies. Of these the most important would naturally be creative composition.

It has always seemed to me illogical that the manu-facture of music should be included in the syllabus as a requirement of academic proficiency. The manufacture of verses is mercifully not considered indispensable to an education in literature. If some of the time spent on learn-ing to manipulate (say) the structure of fugue were spent on listening to and understanding how Buxtehude or Bach used it, the standard of original composition would not deteriorate but improve. That every student, regardless of talent or desire, should be expected to erect specious musical edifices has nothing whatever to do with musical education. Those who have it in them to compose will need no such spurious encouragement; knowledge and love of created music of the past and present will be impetus enough. Those who have no such desire will save their own time and their professor's if they content themselves with learning to be good listeners—an ideal, as we have seen, by no means facile.

Granting that the teaching of composition may be, but is not always, an end worth pursuing, it remains a fact that we teach it not so much with a faulty system as with no system at all. There is a vague inarticulate notion that the method is somehow historical, but it begins, not with plain-song and Ars Antiqua, but with diatonic harmony because (the argument runs) this is the type of music the student has been brought up on. Even here the method lacks logic, since the student has, in fact, been nurtured on late nineteenth-century harmony, which is regarded as too sophisticated a starting-point, so back we go to a kind of harmony resembling that of the simpler four-part Bach chorale. Then we move on to chromatic harmony, and then back to the sixteenth century to acquire a little counterpoint. The process scarcely recommends itself to reason. A case might be made out for maintaining that diatonic harmony is *not* the place to begin, precisely because it is the student's musical bread and butter; and this opinion was proffered in an article on 'Harmony and Composition', published in *Scrutiny* for September, 1939.

Providing that teachers of sufficient imagination and musical understanding could be found, I believe that the method advocated in this previous article (to which the reader is here referred) would be the most rewarding in the teaching of creative composition. With the educational facilities offered by the historical section of the course I have suggested in these pages, particularly the knowledge of the sixteenth-century idiom they would have acquired from the study of that classic among musical text-books, R. O. Morris's *Contrapuntal Technique in the Sixteenth Century,* and from Knud Jeppesen's brilliant hand-book on Palestrina's use of the dissonance, would-be composers will work out their own salvation the more easily if their approach to creative work is by way of melody, polyphony and the human voice. Having a stable traditional background they will gain a clearer understanding of the essentials of musical texture through the creation and combining of original melodic lines, however unpretentious, than they would through years of training in academic harmony and *canto fermo* counterpoint.

The disability of Mr. Rubbra's scheme lies, of course, in the inevitable shortage of truly creative teachers; and this is why, if any more or less rigid system of 'rules' is to be propagated, those of the sixteenth century seem to me the best, because the sixteenth century idiom is the closest approach which music has made to a formalized system evolved from the implications of the human voice and the basic resources of the art of sound. If you dispense with the creative teacher, there is even something to be said for the study of 'strict' text-book counterpoint in so far as it does, as an astonishingly diverse number of authorities ranging from Professor Dent to Roussel, Satie, Hindemith and Krenek have pointed out, encourage fluency and clarity in the manipulation of musical material. It must, however, be clearly understood that *canto fermo* counterpoint can teach no essential discipline that is not implicit in the creative counterpoint advocated by Mr. Rubbra, so long as there are creative teachers capable of offering the student advice. And Holst's objection to the strict system still seems to me to hold. If, he said, the only point of C.F. exercises, which bear no vital relation to the counterpoint of the sixteenth century, is to introduce a 'discipline', then why not apply a different discipline occasionally, for the sake of variety; why not work exercises in which all *concords* are forbidden? This objection need not be as facetious as it sounds : for if this kind of technical training is considered desirable I would certainly advocate that some work should be done on Krenek's twelve-note *Studies in Counterpoint,* whether the young composer has duodecuple aspirations or not[4].

Besides having the same fundamental basis, creative studies would also link up very intimately with historical ones in so far as true creative composition entails always the most scrupulous concern for the material resources of music—the medium one is using and the means whereby 'states' of mind and feeling are to be transmogrified into the stuff of sound. And this brings us to the function of the performer—the last aspect of academic training which I want to discuss.

V

I began this article by deploring the manner in which the manufacture of performers is regarded as perhaps the primary function of musical academies; almost the last point I want to make is that the manufacture of performers should be always seen in relation to wider cultural conceptions. Of course, everyone should acquire sufficient proficiency on an instrument or instruments to enable him to pursue adequately his own musical interests and to educate himself ; but the performances of us all, from clumsy stumblers to virtuosi, would improve if they started from the ability to listen to the music we are trying to perform : to be a great interpreter without having acquired a general musical education is an impossibility. In the first place one needs knowledge and understanding to appre-

4 Since the above was written Hindemith's *Craft of Musical Composition* has appeared in an American edition. It reconciles 'creative' teaching of the kind advocated by Rubbra with a comprehensive theory of tonal relationships which is given scientific sanction. Unfortunately the work is still not easily obtainable in this country.

ciate the composer's intentions; in the second place one needs creative zest of no common order to make these intentions live in actual performance : so that interpretation is always a matter of the subtlest reconciliation of divergent tendencies. How subtle just one example will indicate. One part of the interpreter's task is to present objectively 'the notes as the composer wrote them', yet so clumsy and inadequate a symbolism is musical notation that it requires a creative effort merely to translate the symbols into sound. For instance we are told that expert violinists play neither in just nor in equal temperament but in a mixture of both according to the character of particular passages—melodic scale passages or passages bearing the implications of diatonic harmony. It therefore follows that even 'the notes as the composer wrote them' is no clearly defined ideal; and the problem becomes immensely more complex when we add to the (inevitably) partially personal translation of the would-be objective symbols the entirely personal re-creation of the original experience which is due to the psychological make-up of the performer himself. To be a great interpreter may not call for as important a kind of genius as is necessary to be a great composer : the case of Busoni suggests that it does require genius of a similar order.

That the standard of orchestral players to-day should be higher than it has ever been is, of course, a very fine tribute to our wide-spread instrumental proficiency; yet it cannot be denied that the prodigious number of manually dexterous solo performers has a seamy side with reference to the general conditions of musical taste, in that the more we hear *superficially* convincing performers the more insidiously we grow to be satisfied with the second-rate. It is a remarkable and suggestive fact that to-day, when instrumental technique has never been on a higher *general* level of competence, the art of singing—that which is most intimately connected with the evolution of the organic musical forms—has declined to an abject piti-fulness such as cannot be paralleled in musical history.

About the personal element in performance which only taste and imagination can supply one can say, of course, next to nothing, nor can 'instruction' be given in these qualities. But about the knowledge which should lie behind them one can say a great deal and in the long run this too will depend on taste and on the possession of the historical perspective. It is curious that although no one would venture to perform on the (to us) more esoteric instruments such as the harpsichord or viol without some study of the ways in which the character of the instrument has influenced the idiom of the music written for it, such knowledge is usually regarded as the province of exclusively antiquarian specialists. A comparison of a per-formance on the harpsichord by Wanda Landowska of (say) Bach's 'Chromatic Fantasy and Fugue' with a per-formance of this work—even Edwin Fischer's—on the modern piano establishes once and for all the absurdity of attempting to perform this music on any instrument other than the one for which it was triumphantly com-posed—establishes the harpsichord, moreover, as an instrument utterly different in idiom and sonority from the piano but in no way inferior, indeed in many respects much more magnificent: and no one who has heard Scarlatti or Couperin sensitively played on a harpsichord can fail to appreciate how intimately this music is bound up with its medium—the clear resonance, the precision of line, the metallic percussive effects, the suggestion of a delicate ornamental brush-work—and how sensitive per-formance cannot be achieved without knowledge, an historical basis to one's sympathy and personal interpreta-tion. Yet with music and mediums more familiar how seldom is this the case. How many times is Bach 'inter-preted' with the intensest passion and the best intentions, how seldom is his music played or sung with that knowledge of his *own* intentions—how he wanted his music phrased, in what varying proportions the different sonorities—without which imagination however sincere and fingering however dexterous are merely misplaced energy. Even Chopin, a composer who lends himself naturally to the serpentine 'personal' approach, would be better performed if his interpreters had some notion, which is not impossible of attainment, of how Chopin played his own music and of how he fits into the tradition of European music. (Horowitz, I think, conveys the authentic Chopin impression.)

It often used to be referred to as an instance of the remoteness of academic theory from the living evolution of musical form that students could be put through a complete course of sixteenth-century counterpoint without realizing that the rigid 'rules' they were taught to apply were not an arbitrary systematization which occurred inexplicably at this period of history, but grew naturally out of the facts of song—without realizing, for instance, that discords had to be 'prepared' simply because voices could not, without instrumental aid or the familiarity with harmonic effects that instruments entail, sing notes standing in discordant relation to each other except in so far as they were created by the movement of singable melodic progressions starting from consonance. The work of Morris has perhaps corrected this kind of fallacy; yet it is an instance that is in no wise essentially different from an ignorance that in performers is common-place and passes without comment. It should be obligatory on all intending performers to acquire as a basis for their technical work a general musical cultivation and sufficient knowledge to render their interpretations, if not products of genius, at least worthy of respect.

VI

Musical academies should be the focal points of the musical life of the society that supports them : for this reason I would advocate that among the specialized studies

—composing, interpreting, conducting, and so forth—courses should be offered on Music and the Theatre and Music and the Cinema. The first of these would embrace, of course, some kind of survey of the evolution of opera and ballet, but would be centred in the possible relationship between music and the theatre in the present day, with particular reference to the work in this field of the American composer Marc Blitzstein. In the course on Music and Cinema, students would be able to tackle the essential problems by comparing cinema-scores by Aaron Copland or Hans Eisler with those of the average hack, and the more intelligent and creative criticism of popular functional music that could be encouraged the better the efficiency of the function and the spiritual health of the populace. 'Serious' professional musicians in this country are blithely unconcerned about popular functional music because it is so 'debased'; they forget that only if they bother their high and mighty heads about it is it ever likely to be less so. This is why, despite the poverty of most American creative writing, the work of men like Blitzstein and Copland induces a feeling of hopefulness that it is difficult to experience on this side. I have no doubt that if there is to be a future for music as a social manifestation, musical academies will have to acquire a sense of social responsibility. Music must be an aspect of human life, not the property of the academic or the æsthete.

VII

This point, as well as the one about the prevailing ignorance of performers, is not of merely esoteric interest. The all-pervasiveness of a superficial musical culture to-day—the vast amount of music passively heard, particularly through mechanical means—makes the upholding of the highest musical values more important than it has ever been. We need critical discrimination in music more desperately than in any of the other arts if only because music exerts so insidiously direct an effect on the nervous system. Discrimination means, of course, more sensitive *listening,* and one knows that, if people are too lazy and apathetic to make an effort themselves, one can do nothing to persuade them to listen to music by talking about it because the art is by nature too intangible to render anything one says convincing to those not willing to be convinced. Musical instruction can never do more than give direction to eager and enquiring minds.

But for, at least, these eager and enquiring minds the very hermetic nature of music brings the richest compensations. Precisely because it is, as Roussel said, of all arts the most 'inaccessible', it is the strongest fortress of 'spiritual values' in times when these values are most violently besieged. One should not need to justify further the urgency of musical education, however remote it may seem from 'the present conflict'.

Scrutiny, 1941.

This book is set in 10-pt. Baskerville, a type designed by the calligrapher and printer to the University of Cambridge, John Baskerville (1706-1775) of Birmingham. Baskerville is a classical type-face described as a letter embodying the most precise geometrical proportions with the greatest elegance. Its sharp precision of outline, best seen on a smooth surface paper under ideal conditions of machining, makes it the forerunner of what is now known as the series of ' moderns.'

The present design is the Intertype version. The book is printed directly from the slugs cast on the Intertype machine.